'Round the world cooking library

German Cooking

Savory German dishes prepared in the traditional way

Recipe contributions by Arne Krüger

editor of 'der Feinschmecker'-magazine and author of several cookbooks

DAVID & CHARLES : NEWTON ABBOT

Contents

0 7153 6237 2

Produced by Plenary Publications International, Inc., New York, Amsterdam Office, in the Netherlands for David & Charles (Holdings) Limited
South Devon House – Newton Abbot – Devon

Cup measures in this book are based on an eight ounce cup.

Deutschland am Tisch

Specialities from North Germany against a background of the impressive old Trendelburg Castle.

A word that the Germans themselves use to describe many aspects of German life, is 'gründlich', meaning solid. Like most national characteristics, the German reputation for extreme thoroughness and heavyhanded seriousness has been exaggerated. But no one – and particularly not the Germans themselves – would deny the German passion for organizing everything down to the smallest detail, or their profound distrust of improvisation. This applies not only to their cars and cameras, but to their cooking as well. German cooking may not possess the fantasy and imagination of Italian cooking, or the delicate refinements of French cooking, but this does not mean that German cooking is bad. On the contrary. German home cooking (which the Germans call 'gut bürgerliche Küche', or good plain cooking) is honest, down-to-earth, simple and substantial; it is perfectly in tune with the earnest spirit of German life.
Traditionally, the Germans eat five times a day. But this custom is slowly disappearing as the traditional belly of the honest burgher has given way to the slimmer lines that doctors and the younger generation approve. The day begins, or at any rate used to, with a breakfast consisting of crisp,

fresh 'Semmeln', the famous milk rolls. These are served with butter, honey and a three-minute egg accompanied by a large pot of coffee. In the south of Germany it is accompanied by an equally large pot of tea.

The second breakfast is served at around eleven o'clock. In nobler times, the rich shipowners in Hamburg and Bremen, the aristocrats in their castles, and the stately lords of Berlin, Munich and Frankfurt, made a grand ritual of this meal. It was customary to go to a famous restaurant that served such delicacies as smoked goose breast, smoked salmon, or a plate of oysters with a bottle of white Rhine wine or a bottle of sparkling Sekt, the German version of Champagne. (It is said that Sekt never tastes so marvelous as at eleven o'clock in the morning.)

The common man, for his part, ate hot sausages and potato salad, along with a glass of beer, for his second breakfast; the farmer out in the country ate thick slices of dark bread and cured ham with a few small glasses of brandy called 'schnaps'.

The brandy assumed several different forms from region to region: in the north of Germany, it was a crystal-clear gin which tasted of Kornbrand (corn brandy); in the south of Germany it was either inviting, aromatic Kirschwasser (distilled from stewed cherries) or Zwetschenwasser (distilled from stewed plums). In the country, the second breakfast is still a strictly followed tradition, but in the cities it has been gradually reduced to a simple sausage sandwich which children take to school and adults take to work. By noon the stomach has just barely had time to begin to growl, but it is time for 'Mittagessen', which is actually dinner and a substantial meal. It begins with soup, preferably made with noodles or dumplings, and is followed either by a roast, accompanied by potatoes and vegetables or a salad, by a hearty casserole dish, or by sauerkraut with different kinds of sausages.

At five o'clock, as the afternoon draws to a close, it is time for 'Kaffee mit Kuchen', coffee with cakes and tarts. This 'Kaffee' is the German counterpart of the English 'tea time'. The coffee hour is treated almost like a complete meal.

In old-fashioned German families, the table is set with beautiful lace or embroidered tablecloths and with the best silverware and china. The German housewife puts her heart and soul into these homemade cakes and tarts. Even those who don't happen to be very good cooks are almost invariably good bakers.

In the shopping centers of the large cities and the small towns of the provinces alike, the coffee hour is the most pleasant part of the day. The 'Konditoreien', those renowned pastry shops, fill up with housewives who are out shopping, with couples, and even with men who come alone. Unlike their American counterparts, German men never seem to mind being seen in the genteel atmosphere of a pastry shop enjoying a cup of coffee and a slice of cake. In fact, it is very difficult at the coffee hour to find a seat around one of the small bright tables.

In many German cities, there are famous pastry shops with a tradition that goes back more than 150 years. The shop windows are arranged with cakes, fruit pies, cream pies, and chocolate tarts that could tempt the resolve of a saint. After a day of this much culinary indulgence, it would be surprising if there were much appetite left for the evening meal. An 'Abendbrot', a simple cold meal, is the usual choice. It consists of several kinds of bread accompanied by cold meats and sausages. Often there are also different kinds of cheeses, such as Emmenthaler (commonly known as Swiss cheese, but actually a native of Bavaria). Beer is always the faithful companion. All the ingredients for the 'Abendbrot' are usually bought in the 'Feinkost-geschäfte', better known to us as a delicatessen. The German delicatessen is a unique contribution to good eating, with a bewildering choice of cold meats and sausages, beautifully displayed and deliciously aromatic. These are foods for which Germany is unsurpassed. Of course, the almost mythical American hot dog had its origins among these numerous spicy frankfurters. There are also many different kinds of beer sausages, with or without spices, onions and garlic, but always marvellously tasty. Then there are the many varieties of the appetizing liver sausage: the hearty Berliner sausage and the light Saxon sausage. There are dark blood sausages, sometimes made with kidneys or tongue, and white 'Weisswurst' made with aromatic green garden herbs. There is priceless ham from Westphalia which is smoked over a smoldering juniper berry fire that gives it a particular and distinctive aroma. Besides all these, the delicatessen carries ready-to-serve salads made with meats, creamy potatoes or the delicate meat of a calf's head that has been marinated in sour cream and then minced until smooth and creamy. For those who would rather have fish there are delicacies like

A tall goblet of Rhine wine and a delicious variety of German cheeses: an inseparable union.

Good, hearty, country breads provide the perfect companion for the hundreds of German sausages.

smoked salmon and smoked eel, or Bismarck herring in a sour, piquant sauce. There are also 'Rolmops', which is sour herring wrapped around sour pickles. And if all this weren't enough of a choice for a light supper, there is still cold trout in aspic, or smoked trout, or fine lobster from Helgoland, the small rocky island off the northern coast of Germany.
Apart from their fame in the art of sausage-making, the Germans excel in a number of other gastronomic specialities. One of the first to come to mind is sauerkraut. The Ancient Romans probably knew the principles of how to make it. Finely shredded, salted cabbage was placed in pots or vats allowing a special fermentation to take place which gave the cabbage a slightly sour taste, but left it easily digestible all the same. This art seems to have disappeared from Europe with the fall of the Roman Empire. But it was brought back by the Asiatic hordes who invaded Eastern Europe in the Thirteenth and Fourteenth Centuries. The Asiatic invaders were very well acquainted with the art of making sauerkraut, and since cabbage is one of the hardiest vegetables grown, sauerkraut actually formed the basis for the alimentation of the whole of Eastern and Central Europe, from Rumania to Alsace on the eastern border of France. Today, the area surrounding Stuttgart grows millions of cabbages, all of which will disappear into earthenware and wooden vats for a time, to reappear as aromatic white sauerkraut.
Sauerkraut is a very versatile dish in Germany; it is served in winter and summer, in the humblest kitchens and the best restaurants, with ham, bacon, partridge, goose and with different kinds of sausages. Hot sauerkraut with frankfurters is the traditional snack eaten in train stations and wayside restaurants along the turnpikes and highways.
Another specialty of German cuisine is the delightful assortment of fresh-baked cakes and tarts, and sweet and spiced breads. Gingerbread, honeybread and spiced gingerbread are never absent from any Christmas table.
Every year, a few weeks before Christmas, the Christmas market opens in the cities and small villages. The Christmas tree is put up in the middle of the market square of the picturesque old towns.
Nearby, the grey tower of the cathedral disappears in the December mist, and behind the small windows of the Medieval city hall, glows the golden crown of candles. The market stalls grouped around the Christmas tree sell

Christmas ornaments, flowers and, especially, cookies. Heart or star-shaped, these special cookies taste of honey and spices, are decorated with pink and white sugar borders and have ribbons so that they can be hung in the Christmas tree. According to tradition, each child who goes to the market with his mother or grandmother always returns home carrying one of these cookies around his neck.
German cooking is known for still another specialty, the goose. This has acquired the status of a sort of national fowl. These load cackling birds can almost always be seen walking in long lines through the small German villages. The goose is said to be a difficult fowl to prepare, being too large for one person and too small for two (which gives a good impression of the German appetite). The Germans prepare goose in a number of different ways, but they prefer it stuffed with apples and prumes. Smoked goose breast is an especially refined German delicacy that ranks with smoked salmon and smoked trout. The plentiful goose fat is never wasted. It can be melted and blended with grated apples to make a spread for dark, somewhat sour, farmer's bread, and it is used to fry the most delicious potatoes in the world. One cooking art the Germans fully understand is that of roasting game. Though a crowded country, Germany still has a large reserve of forests and woods, including the famous Black forest, the forests of the Eifel, Hunsrück, the mountain chains of the Weser and the hills of Northern Bavaria. Game, such as deer and wild boar, rabbit and pheasant, still roams these forests freely, and in the wilder forests of Bavaria there are even capercaillie.
Game tastes best when prepared in the old traditional manner: roasted and accompanied by a piquant sauce of wine and spices, by stewed 'Preisselbeeren' (bitter-sour small red berries found in the forest) or by spicy or savory wild brown mushrooms. To really enjoy a game dinner in the authentic fashion, one must go to one of the many old castles. There are still hundreds of them spread all over Germany: old knight's castles and elegant small hunter's castles from the Eighteenth Century. In recent years, the upkeep of these places has become so expensive that many of them have been converted into hotels or restaurants by their owners, whose families and ancestors may have lived there for centuries. In the knights' hall of the castle, a romantic evening is relived just as it took place in the distant past.

The flames dance in the fireplace and the whole hall gives off the aroma of wild game. The table is beautifully decked and wine from the surrounding vineyards sparkles in large goblets. In the small hunters' castles, the guests eat in elegant, cozy dining halls, accompanying their food with plentiful quantities of wine. From gold-framed portraits hanging over the fireplace, ancestral faces in powdered wigs stare down stonily on the strangers sitting around their tables, where fragrant lilies of the valley stand amidst the family silverware and crystal.
Everything served is 'hausgemacht' – homemade – from the inviting berry jam at breakfast and the ham and trout at dinner to the tart at dessert and the plum brandy served with the evening coffee.
Germans love to eat out. One never has to look very far to find a 'Gasthof' an intimate restaurant with a wine or beer cellar. The lovely old handcarved signboard outside points the way for the hungry and thirsty just as it has for centuries. The simple wooden stools covered with checkered cushions are ranged around an unpainted wooden table lit by candles or soft lamplight. The service is in the hands of a stout maiden in a flowered dress and apron who brings beer in large earthenware

mugs, or carries trays laden with glasses of red wine and plates of sauerkraut, sauerbraten or delicious trout. The old German tradition of the 'Stammtisch', the friends' table, still exists in these friendly eating places. Every evening a group of men who know each other exclusively from patronizing other 'Gasthofs' or beer and wine cellars get together to drink and enjoy each other's company. Beer has been the national drink of Germany beyond all memory. German beer, especially Hamburg and Bremen beer, has been famous for centuries. As far back as the Fifteenth and Sixteenth Centuries, it was already being exported to England. Many cities still produce their own beer brewed in the same manner as in the Middle Ages: through natural fermentation which gives it a rich, velvety texture and a distinctive taste. Berlin Weiss (which is flavored with a bit of raspberry juice) and Kölsch are good examples.

In the north of Germany, where the winter is cold and damp, it is customary to warm up with a small glass of 'Schnaps' before starting on the beer. Schnaps is a kind of gin with a strong juniper berry aroma. German beer drinking reaches its apotheosis in the October 'Beer Fest' in Munich. This Bacchanalian festival begins in

One of the castle-hotels near the Neckar river. The cook here serves his guests authentic dishes from the region.

the last week of September and lasts through the first week of October. It takes place in the Theresian meadows, which take their name from the Bavarian princess for whose wedding the feast was first held in 1810. The meadows are usually covered with enormous tents, in which people drink surprising quantities of beer from large earthenware steins – which may hold up to two quarts. These are carried about by buxom 'Mädchen' who manage to deal with four or five of these giants in one hand. Roasted ox, chickens, sausages, and grilled fish are devoured in enormous quantities, the music of street musicians dressed in short leather trousers gets louder and more insistent, and the faces flow redder with beer and the indulgent carnival spirit.

While Germany sometimes seems awash on a sea of beer, we should not forget that it is also a land of wine, where rows of grapevines cling to the sunny southern slopes of hills. There are golden white wines which smell of spring flowers and the blooming apple trees that stand along the edge of the vineyards, and sometimes also of mignonette and hawthorn. There are maiden-like light and fresh Mosel wines, temperamental golden wines of a surprising bouquet from the Rheingau, full-bodied and languid wines from Rheinhesse, luxurious, heady wines from the Rheinpfalz and racy, spicy wines, bottled in flat, round bottles on the shores of the Main. The sparkling wines drunk on the comfortable terraces along the Rhine, under the shade of pruned chestnut trees remain very much in the spirit of Germany's old castles. The delicate golden Rhine wines can still be drunk on the stately white ships that glide through the landscape of hills, forests and castles along the banks of that romantic river. These pale aromatic German wines provide a perfect balance for the solid and serious German cooking.

The best white wines of Germany come from the hills along the Rhine. In the center of this area lies the old town Rüdesheim.

During the wine feasts in September everyone comes to the narrow 'Drosselgasse' with its numerous 'Weinstuben'.

DENMARK
EAST SEA
NORTH SEA
SCHLESWIG-HOLSTEIN
MECKLENBURG
HAMBURG
BREMEN
POLAND
THE NETHERLANDS
NIEDER-
WESER
SACHSEN
BERLIN
BRANDENBURG
ODER
HANNOVER
EAST-GERMANY
ELBE
NEISSE
NORDRHEIN-WESTFALEN
DORTMUND
DÜSSELDORF
WEST-
LEIPZIG
SACHSEN
COLOGNE
BONN
THÜRINGEN
ERFURT
DRESDEN
BELGIUM
AHR
HESSEN
RHEIN
RHEINGAU
FRANKFORT
WÜRZBURG
CZECHOSLOVAKIA
LUXEMBURG
RHEINLAND-PFALZ
MOSEL
MAINZ
RHEINHESSEN
MAIN
GERMANY
NÜRNBERG
WORMS
SAARLAND
DURKHEIM
BAYERN
SPEYER
BADEN-
FRANCE
STUTTGART
DONAU
WÜRTTEMBERG
WINES
MUNICH
SWITZERLAND
RHEIN
AUSTRIA

German Wine

German wines grow principally along the banks of the Rhine and along a few of its tributaries. The great majority are white wines, but there are a few red wines to be found here and there.
From North to South, German wine areas produce the following types:

Ahr

(the towns of Altenahr and Neuenahr): red wines of fairly good quality.

Mosel

(with both tributaries, Saar and Ruwer): simple to very good white wines. The best Mosel wine comes from the area between the villages of Neumagen and Traben-Trarbach.

Rhine

the best known wine areas are:
Mittelrhein (between Sankt Goar and Assmannshausen): white wines of fair to rather good quality;
red wines from the area near Assmannshausen.
Rheingau (between Rüdesheim and Hochheim): white wines which are sometimes of exceptionally good quality. The best German wines come from this area, for example, Schloss Johannisberg and Schloss Vollrads. In England, Rhine wines are often called 'Hock'; the name derives from the wine village, Hochheim, which provided the wines that Queen Victoria loved.
Rheinhessen (between Mainz and Worms): fairly strong white wines of fair quality; red wines from Inghelheim.
Rheinpfalz (between Worms and Speyer): heady white wines mostly of fair quality, but some of very good quality, such as those from the area near Dürkheim.

Main

Most of the wines from this area, and especially from the area surrounding Würzburg, are called 'Frankenweine', good white wines. They arrive at the wine shops in flat, round bottles.

German Beer

Beer is brewed throughout Germany – even small provincial towns have their own breweries. A few of the exceptional beers:
Märzenbier: a light, golden-brown and lively-flavored beer which comes mostly from Munich.
Berliner Weiss: a light beer brewed from wheat through natural fermentation.
Altbier: a racy beer brewed through natural fermentation. It comes principally from Westfalen and Cologne.
Münchener: a fairly strong, dark beer from Munich.
Bockbier: dark, strong, and very aromatic beer which originally came from the small town of Einböck but is now brewed all over Germany.
Dortmunder: light, lively hop beer which comes from Dortmund.

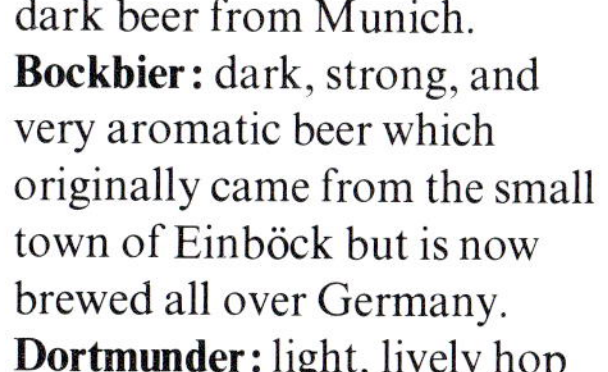

Salted herring and apple salad

Hamburger Heringstöpfchen

Salted herring and apple salad

4 servings

- ½ *cup sour cream*
- 1½ *teaspoons vinegar*
- 1½ *teaspoons sugar*
- ½ *teaspoon horseradish*
- 1 *(5 oz.) jar pickled herring, drained and chopped*
- 1 *medium onion, chopped*
- 1 *apple, peeled, cored and chopped*
- *Lettuce leaves*
- *Pimiento strips*

Combine sour cream, vinegar, sugar and horseradish; blend well. Let stand 10 minutes. Combine herring, onion, apple and pickles; toss lightly. Add dressing; mix lightly. Chill. Serve on lettuce leaves. Garnish with strips of pimiento.

Roter Heringssalat

Salted herring and red beet salad

4 servings

- 4 *(1 lb. jar) salted or schmalz herring fillets cut into ½″ cubes*
- ½ *cup diced cold cooked veal or chicken*
- 1 *(1 lb.) jar pickled beets, drained and chopped*
- 1 *cup diced dill pickles*
- ¼ *cup finely chopped onion*
- 2 *apples, peeled, cored and diced*
- 2 *hard cooked eggs, 1 chopped, 1 sliced*
- ¼ *cup mayonnaise*
- ⅓ *cup light cream*
- 1 *teaspoon pepper*
- 1 *tablespoon sugar*
- 2 *tomatoes, cut into wedges*

In a large bowl, combine fish, meat, beets, pickles, onion, apples and the chopped egg. In a small bowl, blend mayonnaise, cream, pepper and sugar. Combine with fish mixture, place in refrigerator and let stand several hours to blend flavors. Arrange on individual salad plates or in a salad bowl, and garnish with egg slices and tomato wedges. Serve with bread sticks or fresh rolls.

Salted herring and red beet salad

Sausage and onion salad (recipe page 17, 4th column)

The most tempting and enticing sight in Germany is the spacious, festively lit window of the delicatessen, where the salads are artfully displayed.
There is a delightful choice of potato salads, meat salads with sausages, salads with fish and different sorts of vegetable salads. All these are served at the 'Abendbrot', the evening meal of cold cuts and salads which is customary in Germany.
Whether by accident or design, salads are the perfect companion for the substantial, nutritious, dark brown German bread, and for the foamy glass of beer that completes the inseparable trio.
German salads are hardly the light little trifles that the French serve with their food. Nor are they the cold, crisp fresh snacks that we eat as a side dish.
John Barrymore's famous remark that 'there are two things that a woman can make out of nothing: a hat and a salad' has nothing to do with the German variety. The Germans eat their salads as a real meal and expect them to be substantial enough to be worth the effort. And, in contrast to ourselves, the Germans love soft, velvety salads. Nowhere else in the world can you get such creamy potato salads and meat salads as in Germany. The secret of this velvety smoothness is thick sour cream.

Hering in saurer Sahne

Herring in sour cream

4 servings

- *1 cup sour cream*
- *2 tablespoons vinegar*
- *½ teaspoon sugar*
- *1 medium onion, cut into rings*
- *2 (5 oz.) jars herring in wine sauce, drained*

Combine sour cream, vinegar and sugar; blend well. Add onion. Arrange herring on serving dishes. Spoon sour cream mixture over herring.

Kartoffelsalat

Potato salad

6 servings

- *1 cup sour cream*
- *½ cup mayonnaise*
- *1 onion, finely chopped*
- *1 tablespoon vinegar*
- *1 tablespoon prepared mustard*
- *2–3 teaspoons salt*
- *1 teaspoon sugar*
- *⅛ teaspoon black pepper*
- *2 pounds small white potatoes*
- *1 small cucumber, peeled and chopped*
- *8 radishes, sliced*
- *2 carrots, grated*
- *2 hard cooked eggs, sliced*
- *1 tomato, sliced*
- *Chopped parsley*

Combine sour cream, mayonnaise, onion, vinegar, mustard, salt, sugar and pepper; let stand 10–15 minutes. Cook unpeeled potatoes in boiling water until fork-tender about 20–25 minutes. Peel; cut into thin slices. Combine potatoes, cucumber, radishes and carrots in large bowl. Add sour cream mixture; toss lightly. Garnish with eggs, tomato and parsley. Salad may be served hot or cold.

Büsumer Schnittchen

Büsum slices

4 servings

- *4 eggs*
- *½ teaspoon salt*
- *¼ teaspoon paprika*
- *2 tablespoons chopped chives*
- *2 tablespoons margarine or butter*
- *1 medium onion, chopped*
- *1 (4½-oz.) can shrimp*
- *4 slices buttered rye or pumpernickel bread, toasted*
- *4 dill gherkin slices*
- *4 tomato slices*

Beat together eggs, salt, paprika, and chives. Melt margarine in skillet. Add onions and cook until transparent. Stir in shrimp and cook until heated. Pour egg mixture over onion and shrimp; scramble, stirring slowly. Serve on toast while still warm. Garnish with dill gherkin and tomato slices

Wurstsalat

Sausage and onion salad

4 servings

- *4 tablespoons oil*
- *5 teaspoons vinegar*
- *1 teaspoon sugar*
- *½ teaspoon salt*
- *⅛ teaspoon black pepper*
- *½ pound bologna or luncheon meat, thinly sliced*
- *2 dill pickles, chopped*
- *2 stalks celery, chopped*
- *1 medium onion, cut into rings*
- *1 green pepper, chopped*
- *1 cup cooked peas*
- *Lettuce leaves*

Combine oil, vinegar, sugar, salt and black pepper in small jar; shake well to blend. Combine meat, pickles, celery, onion, green pepper and peas; toss lightly. Add dressing; toss lightly. Chill at least 20 minutes. Serve on lettuce leaves.

Hamburger Rundstück

Cold roast sandwiches

4 open-faced sandwiches

- *2 tablespoons mayonnaise*
- *1 tablespoon yogurt*
- *2 tablespoons fresh chopped herbs (parsley, chives, savory) or 2 teaspoons mixed dried herbs*
- *Salt, to taste*
- *Pepper, to taste*
- *4 slices bread, toasted and buttered, if desired*
- *4 lettuce leaves*
- *8 thin slices cold roast veal or pork*
- *Crabapples*
- *Parsley*

Combine mayonnaise, yogurt, and herbs. Season with salt and pepper. Chill. Arrange lettuce leaves on toast. Top with 2 slices trimmed roast pork or veal on each slice. Spread sauce on meat. Cut in half. Garnish with crabapples and parsley.

Schwetzinger Spargelsalat

Asparagus and chicken salad

4 servings

- *4 tablespoons mayonnaise*
- *1 teaspoon vinegar*
- *1 tablespoon parsley flakes*
- *½ teaspoon salt*
- *½ teaspoon sugar*
- *1½ cups cold, cubed, cooked chicken*
- *1 cup pineapple chunks, drained*
- *2 tomatoes, seeded and diced*
- *2 (8½ oz.) cans asparagus pieces, drained*

Combine mayonnaise, vinegar, parsley, salt and sugar; mix lightly; let stand 5–10 minutes. Combine chicken, pineapple and tomatoes in bowl. Add dressing mix; toss lightly. Arrange half the asparagus in salad bowl; pile chicken mix on top. Garnish with remaining asparagus.

Käse Schnitte

Cheese sandwich

6 servings

- *1 large onion, finely chopped*
- *2 teaspoons salad oil*
- *1 teaspoon vinegar*
- *¼ teaspoon salt*
- *6 slices pumpernickel bread*
- *Margarine or butter*
- *Limburger or cream cheese*
- *Freshly ground black pepper*

Combine onion, oil vinegar and salt; let stand 10 minutes. Spread bread generously with margarine, then cheese. Spoon onion mixture over cheese; sprinkle with pepper.

Bremer Salat

Bremen salad

4 servings

- *½ cup sour cream*
- *¼ cup mayonnaise*
- *½ teaspoon curry powder*
- *1 (5 oz.) jar pickled herring, diced*
- *¼ pound luncheon meat, diced*
- *1 apple, peeled, cored and diced*
- *2 stalks celery, diced*
- *1 dill pickle, diced*
- *Lettuce*

Combine sour cream, mayonnaise and curry powder; blend well. Let stand 5–10 minutes. Add remaining ingredients; toss lightly. Chill. Serve on lettuce.

Champignons Salat

Mushroom salad

6 servings

- 1 *pound fresh mushrooms, sliced*
- 4 *sweet gherkin pickles, finely chopped*
- 2 *tablespoons minced onion*
- 1 *clove garlic, minced*
- 1 *tomato, finely chopped*
- ½ *cup salad oil*
- ¼ *cup vinegar*
- ½ *teaspoon sugar*
- 6 *lettuce cups*

Combine mushrooms, pickles onion, garlic and tomato; toss lightly. Add oil, vinegar and sugar; toss lightly until mushrooms are well coated. Chill at least 2 hours. Serve in lettuce cups.

Rheinischer Weihnachtssalat

Rhenish Christmas salad

6 servings

3 cups cold cooked potatoes, cubed
2 cups diced apples
½ cup finely chopped onion
1 cup cold roast veal or chicken
¼ pound cubed ham or pork roll
½ cup cubed sour pickles
1 pickled herring fillet, cubed
¼ cup walnuts, coarsely chopped
¾ cup water
1 tablespoon vinegar
1 teaspoon salt
1 teaspoon sugar
½ cup mayonnaise
1 cup sour cream
2 hard-cooked eggs, sliced
Chopped parsley

Combine potatoes, apples, onion, veal, ham, pickles, herring and walnuts in a large bowl; toss lightly. Sprinkle with water, vinegar, salt and sugar; blend well. Stir together mayonnaise and sour cream; blend into potato mixture. Chill. Serve garnished with egg slices and chopped parsley.

Rote-Beten-Salat

Beet and endive salad

4 servings

1 (8 oz.) can sliced beets
2 Belgian endives, sliced and cut up or 1 small head of chicory, broken into small pieces
1 apple, grated
1 small onion, chopped
2 tablespoons horshradish
2 egg yolks
1 tablespoon lemon juice
3 tablespoons sour cream
½ teaspoon prepared mustard
1 teaspoon sugar
1 teaspoon salt
¼ teaspoon black pepper
½ clove garlic, minced
3 tablespoons oil

In a large salad bowl, combine beets, endive (or chicory), apple, onion, and horseradish. In a small bowl, mix egg yolks, lemon juice, sour cream, mustard, sugar, salt, pepper, and garlic. Mix well. Using a wire whisk, slowly add oil, drop by drop, to dressing mixture. Blend thoroughly. Pour over salad; toss well. Chill.

Krautsalat

Shredded cabbage salad

4 servings

2 cups water
1 teaspoon salt
4 cups shredded cabbage (1 small head cabbage)
1 teaspoon caraway seed
4 slices bacon, diced
1 medium onion, chopped
¼ cup vinegar

Bring water, with salt added, to a boil. Add cabbage and caraway seed. Simmer for 10 minutes; drain and cool. Cook bacon in skillet until lightly browned. Add onions and cook until golden. Add bacon pieces, onions, 4 tablespoons of bacon drippings, and vinegar to cabbage. Toss until well mixed. Serve immediately.

Sauerkrautsalat

Sauerkraut salad

4 servings

1 (16-oz.) can sauerkraut, drained
2 green apples, peeled and chopped
½ cup chopped sour pickles
1 medium onion, chopped
2 tablespoons chopped fresh dill
2 tablespoons chopped parsley
1 teaspoon salt
2 tablespoons sugar
2 tablespoons lemon juice
¼ cup salad oil

Put sauerkraut in salad bowl; separate with fork. Add apples, pickles, onion, dill, parsley, salt, sugar, and lemon juice. Mix well. Heat oil and pour over salad; it should sizzle. Toss until well mixed. Chill. Serve cold.

Schwetzinger Eiergericht

Swetzing molded eggs

4 servings

4 cooked asparagus tips, cut into 1″ pieces
4 eggs
½ teaspoon salt
⅛ teaspoon pepper
⅛ teaspoon paprika
2 tablespoons water
2 tablespoons melted margarine or butter

Place 4 asparagus pieces into each of 4 greased custard cups. Beat eggs with salt, pepper, paprika and water. Pour into prepared custard cups. Carefully pour melted margarine on surface of egg mixture. Place cups in a skillet. Pour boiling water into the pan to a depth of 1″ on the custard cups. Cover and heat in hot water (do not let water boil) until egg mixture is firm, about 20–30 minutes. When sharp knife is inserted in center and comes out clean, custards are done. Serve hot or cold, unmolded from custard cups.

Sauces

Mustard is so important to German cooking that many sauces use it as a base. Mustard is the best friend of pork, and given the immense popularity of pork products in Germany, the mustard pot is almost always on the table.
Mustard is an ancient herb. The Roman legions took it with them throughout Europe. Under the primitive conditions of Europe's Dark Ages, where many of the arts of civilization had been lost, mustard was very popular for preserving the freshness of meat and fish.
Basically, mustard consists of seeds from the mustard plant, which are ground to a fine powder (in the old days with a large stone crusher) and mixed with vinegar and spices. Mustard used to be prepared with sour grape juice, hence the name 'most', meaning unfermented grapejuice.
There are many different varieties of mustard in Germany, some stronger than others, some prepared with wine vinegar, some with beer vinegar and some with fresh green herbs. For fish the Germans use a very light mustard, made from white mustard seeds, and a somewhat darker mustard is used to accompany beer sausages.
Mustard is also used in German cooking to give certain sauces more body and in the preparation of braised meat and game. Meat that has been rubbed with mustard becomes deliciously tender when braised: the sharp flavor of the mustard disappears and only the aroma remains.

Senfsauce

Medium mustard sauce

Makes 2 cups

- *4 tablespoons margarine or butter*
- *4 tablespoons flour*
- *1–2 tablespoons dry mustard*
- *1 teaspoon sugar*
- *2 cups beef bouillon*

Melt margarine in saucepan over low heat. Add flour, mustard and sugar; stir until blended smooth. Slowly add bouillon, stirring constantly to avoid lumps. Cook, stirring until smooth and thickened. For thick sauce increase flour to ½ cup.

Specksauce

Bacon sauce

Makes 2 cups

- *½ pound lean bacon, diced*
- *1 medium onion, chopped*
- *5 tablespoons flour*
- *2 cups beef bouillon*
- *1 teaspoon vinegar*

Fry out bacon in heavy saucepan. Add onion; cook until onion is transparent. Drain off fat; return 2 tablespoons to saucepan. Add flour; stir until blended smooth. Slowly add bouillon and vinegar, stirring constantly to avoid lumps. Cook, stirring until smooth and thickened.

Semmelkren

Horseradish and bread sauce

Makes 2 cups

- *2 cups beef bouillon*
- *½ cup prepared horseradish*
- *2 slices white bread, crusts removed and cubed*
- *1 tablespoon cornflour*
- *2 tablespoons water*
- *½ cup light cream*
- *½ cup sour cream*

Combine bouillon, horseradish and bread in saucepan; bring to a boil. Reduce heat; simmer 5–8 minutes or until bread dissolves. Mix cornflour and water; stir into bouillon mixture. Cook, stirring constantly, until thickened. Stir in cream and sour cream; heat.

Kalte Schnittlauchsauce

Cold chive sauce

Makes 1 cup

- *2 (3 oz.) packages cream cheese and chives*
- *2 teaspoons chives*
- *¼ teaspoon salt*
- *Dash black pepper*
- *¼ cup milk*

Cream together cheese, chives, salt and pepper. Gradually stir in milk; blend until smooth.

Frankfurter grüne Sauce

Herb sauce

Makes 1 cup

- *1 (8 oz.) package plain yogurt, chilled*
- *¼ cup mayonnaise*
- *½ teaspoon dill weed*
- *½ teaspoon dried chervil*
- *½ teaspoon parsley flakes*
- *½ teaspoon chives*
- *¼ teaspoon salt*
- *⅛ teaspoon black pepper*
- *2 hard cooked eggs, chopped*

Combine yogurt, mayonnaise and seasonings; blend well. Stir in chopped egg.

Süddeutscher Salat

South German salad dressing

Makes ½ cup

- *1 small onion, quartered*
- *2 tablespoons chopped parsley*
- *2 tablespoons chopped chives*
- *2 tablespoons boiling water*
- *2 tablespoons vinegar*
- *4 tablespoons salad oil*
- *1 teaspoon prepared mustard*
- *½ teaspoon salt*
- *¼ teaspoon black pepper*

Combine all ingredients in blender jar; blend smooth.

Soups

The word soup is linguistically linked with the German word 'saufen', meaning to drink abundantly. Which may help to explain why every German loves soup and no German lunch is complete without it. There is a soup for every occasion and practically every day of the year in Germany. Germany has a continental climate with fairly cold winters. A snowy day calls for a hearty, well-seasoned soup, preferably made with peas or beans, with a thick pig's foot and a variety of herbs. The glass of beer that follows tastes as good as it ever will. If something more filling is required there is a soup with 'Knödel', which are dumplings made with flour and sometimes blended with ground liver.

But if soup is just the beginning of a long festive dinner (and one must be careful not to spoil the appetite for the good things still to come) then a delicious 'Fleischbrühe' is ladled out. This is a tasty, clear broth prepared very slowly from meat and bones and then richly seasoned with fresh garden herbs. On a hot summer's day the Germans make a delicous cold fruit soup from cherries that quenches all thirst and conquers all lethargy.

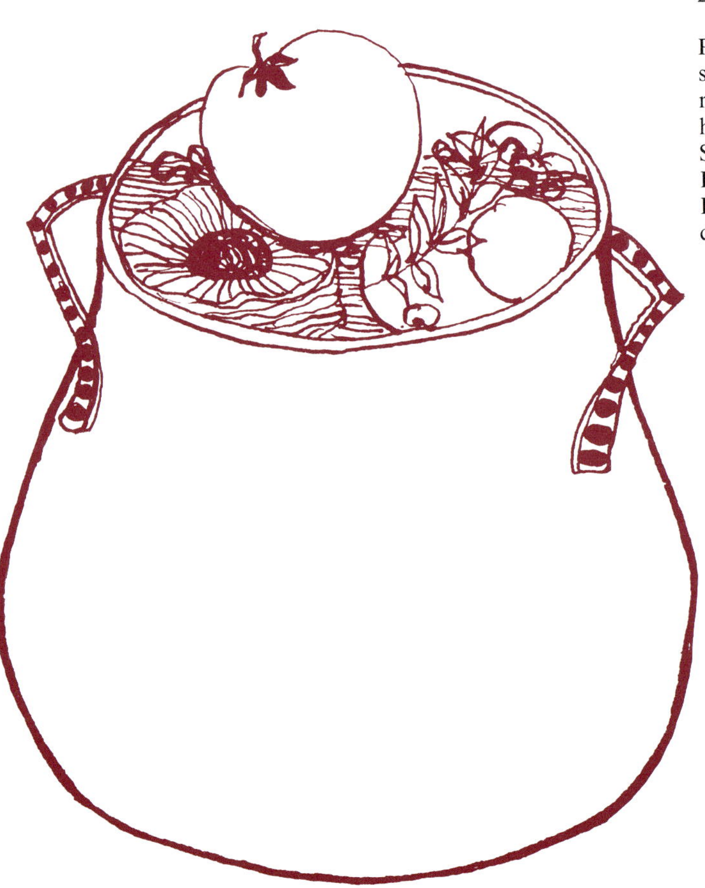

Fleischbrühe

Beef broth

6 servings

3 pounds shin of beef with bone
1 large onion, chopped
2 carrots, chopped
1 stalk celery, chopped
1 sprig parsley, chopped
1 tablespoon salt
2 bay leaves
4 juniper berries, optional
8 peppercorns, crushed
2½ quarts water

Place all ingredients in large saucepot. Bring to a boil; reduce heat; simmer 2–2½ hours or until meat is tender. Skim off foam as it appears. Remove from heat; strain. Remove meat from bone and chop coarsely; return to broth.

Ochsenschwanzsuppe

Oxtail soup

6–8 servings

2 pounds oxtails, well trimmed
2 medium onions, cut into wedges
1 large carrot, quartered
2 cups celery tops, about 3″ pieces
1 teaspoon salt
¼ teaspoon pepper
4 cloves or allspice berries
2 quarts water
1 carrot, peeled and diced
1 parsnip or small turnip, peeled and diced
2 slices boiled ham, diced
2 cups fine noodles, lightly packed

Place oxtails, onion, quartered carrot, celery, salt, pepper, cloves, and water in large kettle. Cover. Bring to a boil; reduce heat; simmer about 4 hours or until meat is loosened from bones. Strain; discard vegetables. Remove meat from bones; dice. Measure liquid; add water to make 8 cups. Bring to a boil; add diced carrots and parsnips; boil about 10 minutes. Add oxtail meat, ham and noodles. Cook until noodles are just tender, about 5 minutes.

Betenbartsch

Beet soup

8 servings

3 pound beef shank with bones
2 quarts water
1 large onion, chopped
1 stalk celery, chopped
1 sprig parsley, chopped
1 tablespoon salt
2 (1 lb.) cans beets, drained and diced
1 cup sour cream
4 tablespoons flour
1 teaspoon sugar
2 teaspoons vinegar
¼ teaspoon dried marjoram

Place meat in large saucepan. Add water, onion, celery, parsley and salt. Bring to a boil; reduce heat; simmer 1½–2 hours. Remove meat. Strain broth. Combine broth and beets in saucepan. Bring just to a boil. Combine remaining ingredients. Stir into hot beet mixture. Continue to cook over low heat, stirring constantly, until slightly thickened. Dice meat and add to soup.

Nürnberger Gemüsesuppe

Nurnberg vegetable soup

6 servings

2 (10¾ oz.) cans vegetable soup with beef
1 (10½ oz.) can beef bouillon
1 soup can water
1 teaspoon dried chervil
¼ cup sour cream

Combine soup, bouillon, water and chervil in saucepan. Bring to a boil; reduce heat. Stir in sour cream. Serve.

Kartoffelsuppe

Potato soup

4–6 servings

2 (10-½ oz.) cans chicken consommé
1 soup can water
2 cups diced potatoes
2 scallions, chopped
1 soup can milk
1 teaspoon Worcestershire sauce
½ cup sour cream

Combine consommé, water, potatoes and scallions in large saucepan; bring to a boil. Reduce heat; simmer until potatoes are tender, about 12 minutes. Blend smooth in blender or press through fine sieve; return to saucepan. Stir in milk and Worcestershire sauce; heat. Stir in sour cream. Serve hot or well chilled.

Liver dumpling soup. Eating a bowl of soup with a large slippery dumpling in it requires just a little bit of caution. The most practical way to proceed is to carefully break the dumpling up with your spoon and then stir it into the soup.

Leberknödelsuppe

Liver dumpling soup

4 servings

¼ *pound beef liver*
1 *egg*
2 *tablespoons melted margarine or butter*
¾ *cup fine bread crumbs*
1 *small onion, finely chopped*
1 *teaspoon parsley flakes*
¼ *teaspoon dried marjoram*
¼ *teaspoon salt*
4 *cups beef bouillon*

Remove membranes from liver. Mince finely or chop in blender. Combine liver, egg, margarine, bread crumbs, parsley, marjoram and salt; mix well. Chill about 25–30 minutes. Bring bouillon to a boil. Form meat mixture into 4 meatballs. Drop meatballs into simmering bouillon. Cook 10 minutes. Serve meatballs with bouillon in large soup bowls.

A good leek soup is made by using not only the white part of the leek, but also the tender yellow-green part (recipe page 29, 1st column).

Krabben Bisque

Shrimp bisque

4 servings

- 2 *($10\frac{1}{2}$ oz.) cans cream of shrimp soup*
- 1 *soup can milk*
- ½ *pound shrimp, shelled and cleaned*
- ¼ *teaspoon fennel seed, crushed*
- ¼ *teaspoon dill weed*
- 1 *cup heavy cream*

Combine soup and milk in saucepan; stir until well blended. Add shrimp, fennell and dill. Cook over medium heat, stirring constantly, until heated. Slowly stir in cream; heat. Serve immediately.

Badische Lauchsuppe

Baden leek soup

6–8 servings

4 leeks
½ cup margarine or butter
2 large onions, chopped
6 cups water
6 chicken bouillon cubes
½ teaspoon salt
1 cup milk
1 cup finely chopped ham, optional

Slice leeks lengthwise; wash thoroughly under running water; cut into 1″ pieces. Melt margarine in heavy saucepan; sauté leeks and onions until leeks are soft. Add water, bouillon cubes, and salt. Bring to a boil; reduce heat; simmer 8–10 minutes, stirring occasionally. Add milk; heat. Ladle soup into serving dishes; sprinkle with chopped ham.

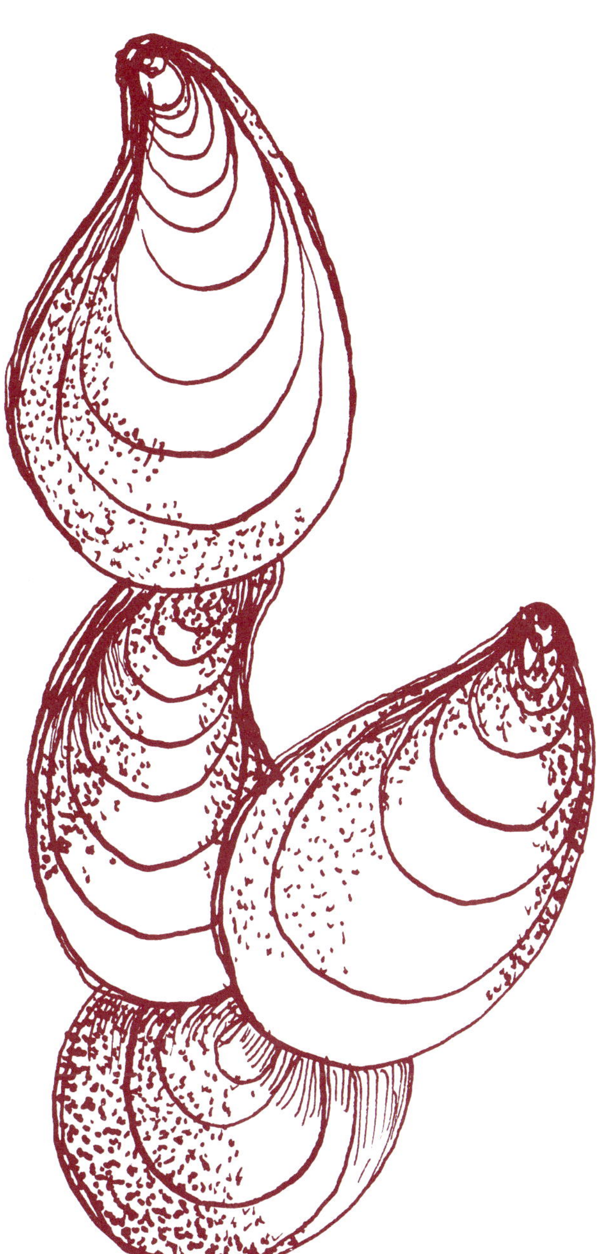

Muschelsuppe

Mussel chowder

4 servings

2 pounds mussels or clams in shell
¼ cup water
3 slices bacon, diced
2 medium onions, chopped
1 stalk celery, chopped
3 medium potatoes, peeled and cubed
1 teaspoon salt
⅛ teaspoon black pepper
2 cups milk
Margarine or butter

Wash and scrub mussels. Place mussels in large saucepot with the water. Cook just until shells open. Strain; reserve liquid. Remove mussels from shells and chop coarsely.
In heavy saucepot fry out bacon. Sauté onions and celery until onions are transparent. Add potatoes, salt, pepper and 1 cup mussel broth. Cook until potatoes are tender about 15–20 minutes. Stir in milk and mussels; heat. Top each serving of chowder with a generous pat of margarine.

This hearty Westerland fish soup with bread is a complete meal in itself.

Westerländer Fischsuppe

Fish soup

6–8 servings

- ¼ *cup margarine or butter*
- 4 *medium onions, chopped*
- 2 *(1 lb.) packages frozen fish fillets, cut into bite size pieces*
- 2 *medium potatoes, cubed*
- 4 *cups water*
- 2 *(8 oz.) bottles clam juice*
- 4 *tomatoes, peeled and quartered*
- 1 *cup broad noodles*
- ¼ *cup cooked diced bacon, drained*
- ¼ *pound shrimp, shelled and cleaned*
- 1 *small cucumber, peeled and chopped*
- 1 *teaspoon parsley flakes*
- 1 *pound mussels or clams, in shells*

Melt margarine in large heavy saucepan. Sauté onions until transparent. Add fish, potatoes and water. Bring to a boil; reduce heat; simmer 15 minutes. Add clam juice, tomatoes and noodles; simmer 8–10 minutes. Stir in bacon, shrimp, cucumber and parsley. Add mussels. Cook just until mussel shells open.

Buttermilchsuppe

Buttermilk soup

4–6 servings

- 3 *tablespoons cornflour*
- 4 *cups buttermilk*
- 1 *tablespoon chives*
- 1 *teaspoon salt*
- 1 *egg yolk*
- 1 *hard cooked egg, chopped*

Stir cornflour into buttermilk until smooth. Cook over medium heat, stirring constantly, until thick. Stir in salt and chives. Beat a small amount of hot mixture into egg; return to buttermilk mixture; stir well. Serve hot. Garnish with chopped egg.

Ostpreußische Brotsuppe

East Prussian bread soup

4 servings

- 8 *slices white bread, crusts removed and cubed*
- 4 *cups water*
- 4 *cloves*
- 1 *stick cinnamon*
- 1 *tablespoon sugar*
- ½ *teaspoon salt*
- ½ *cup sour cream*
- 1 *tablespoon lemon juice*

Combine bread, water, cloves, cinnamon, sugar and salt in saucepan. Bring to a boil; reduce heat; simmer 15 minutes. Strain. Heat; stir in sour cream and lemon juice.

Biersuppe

Beer soup

4 servings

2 cups milk
1 stick cinnamon
1 piece lemon peel, 1″ wide
1 tablespoon sugar
2 tablespoons cornflour
¼ cup cold water
1 (12 oz.) can beer
1 egg yolk, slightly beaten

In saucepan, combine milk, cinnamon, lemon peel and sugar; bring to a boil. Reduce heat; simmer 10 minutes. Dissolve cornflour in cold water; stir into milk mixture. Continue to cook, stirring constantly, until thickened. Stir in beer; heat. Beat a small amount of hot beer mixture into egg; return to saucepan. Stir well. Remove from heat; strain. Serve hot or cold.

Hamburger Kirschkaltschale

Hamburg cold cherry soup

6–8 servings

2 (16 oz.) cans sour pitted cherries in water
1 cup sugar
1 stick cinnamon
1 tablespoon cornflour
2 tablespoons water
Crushed macaroons, optional

Combine cherries and liquid, sugar, and cinnamon in saucepan; stir well. Bring to a boil; reduce heat; simmer 10 minutes. Press through fine sieve; return to saucepan; heat. Dissolve cornflour in cold water; stir into hot mixture. Continue to cook, stirring constantly, until thickened. Serve hot or well chilled. Sprinkle with crushed macaroons before serving.

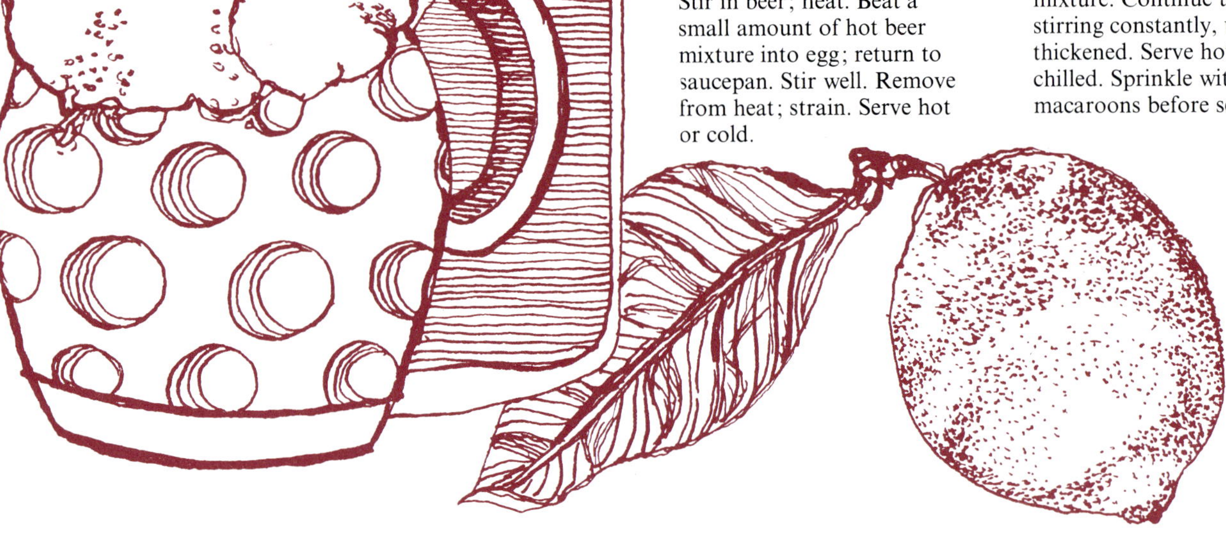

The Pfalz region is the great wine cellar of Germany and, of course, the region where you would expect them to know how to make a good wine soup.

Pfälzer Rotweinsuppe

Red wine soup

4 servings

2 cups dry red wine
2 cups water
4 tablespoons minute tapioca
2 tablespoons sugar
½ stick cinnamon
1 piece lemon peel, ½″ thick
2 egg whites
1 tablespoon sugar
Ladyfingers or sweet wafers

Combine wine, water, tapioca, sugar, cinnamon and lemon peel in saucepan. Bring to a boil; reduce heat; simmer 8–10 minutes, stirring frequently. Beat egg whites until soft peaks form. Gradually beat in sugar; beating until stiff. Strain soup. Top each serving of soup with "icebergs" of egg white. Serve hot.

Fish dishes

Ostpreußische Bierfische

Fish in beer, East Prussian style

6 servings

2 cups water
1 (12 oz.) bottle dark beer
1 tablespoon finely chopped parsley
½ cup celery, chopped
1 medium onion, chopped
2 teaspoons salt
1 teaspoon pickling spice
1 teaspoon margarine or butter
3 tablespoons cornflour carp or pike, cut into serving pieces
3 tablespoons cornflour
¼ cup water
1 teaspoon lemon juice
Sugar
Parsley sprigs

Combine water, beer, parsley, celery, onion, salt, pickling spice, and margarine in large skillet or wide saucepan. Bring to boiling point; do not allow to boil. Add fish pieces. Poach until fish flakes easily when tested with fork, about 3–5 minutes, depending on thickness of pieces. Carefully remove fish to heated platter with slotted spoon. Strain broth. Combine cornflour and water. Add to broth. Bring to a boil and cook until thickened, stirring constantly. Add lemon juice. Season to taste with a little sugar. Serve fish and sauce separately with boiled potatoes. Garnish with parsley sprigs.

Ratsherren-Fisch

"Councillors" fish

4 servings

1½ pounds frozen fish fillets, thawed
½ teaspoon salt
¼ teaspoon black pepper
¼ cup margarine or butter, melted
¼ cup milk
1 tablespoon flour
⅔ cup grated cheddar cheese
1 tablespoon snipped parsley

Place fish fillets in buttered shallow casserole (7″ × 10″). Sprinkle with salt and pepper. Pour melted margarine over fillets. Bake in a hot oven (400°) for 15–20 minutes or until fish flakes when tested with fork. Mix milk, flour, and cheese together. Pour over fillets and return them to oven until top is browned, about 10–12 minutes. Sprinkle with parsley.

Wriezener Makrelen

Poached mackerel with herbs

4 servings

4 whole mackerel, cleaned
1 tablespoon vinegar
1 teaspoon salt
¼ teaspoon black pepper
1 onion, quartered
½ cup water
1 cup white wine
3 peppercorns, crushed
½ bay leaf
1 whole clove
½ teaspoon thyme
2 tablespoons cornflour
¼ cup water
½ cup cream
2 tablespoons margarine or butter
1½ tablespoons chopped chives
1½ tablespoons chopped parsley

Sprinkle fish with vinegar, salt, and pepper. In large skillet mix onion, water, wine, peppercorns, bay leaf, clove, and thyme; bring to a boil Carefully add fish; reduce heat and cover. Poach for 15–20 minutes or until fish flakes when tested with fork. Remove fish and keep warm. Strain fish broth; measure 1 cup. Return to skillet. Blend cornflour into cold water; add fish broth. Cook until thickened and clear. Stir in cream, margarine, chives and parsley. Serve hot over fish.

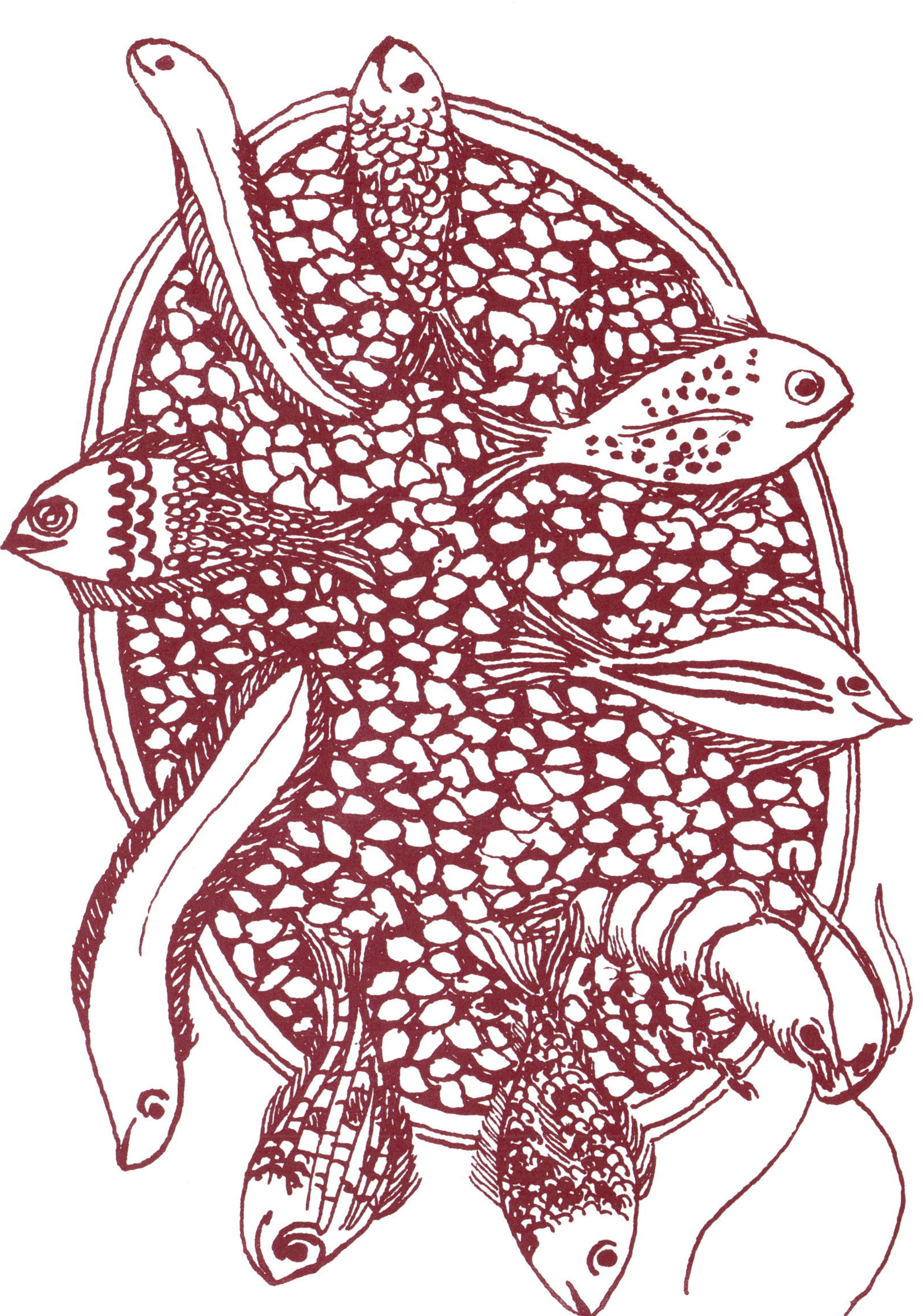

Hamburger Kasserolle

Fish casserole

6 servings

- 2 *tablespoons margarine or butter*
- 1 *medium onion, chopped*
- 1 *(16 oz.) package frozen fish fillets, cut into bite-size pieces*
- ½ *pound scallops*
- ½ *pound shrimp, shelled and cleaned*
- 1 *(10 oz.) package frozen artichoke hearts, thawed*
- 1 *(3 oz.) can sliced mushrooms, drained*
- 1 *(10½ oz.) can mushroom soup*
- 1 *cup dry white wine*
- ½ *teaspoon salt*
- 2 *cups cooked rice*
- 2 *teaspoons parsley flakes*
- 2 *tablespoons grated Parmesan cheese*

Melt margarine in large skillet; sauté onion in margarine until transparent. Add fish, scallops, shrimp, artichoke hearts, mushrooms, soup, wine and salt; mix well. Combine rice and parsley in greased 2½ qt. casserole. Pour fish mixture over rice. Bake in a moderate oven (350°) 20 minutes. Sprinkle cheese over top; bake 10 minutes longer.

Fish stew Büsum style. Grated horseradish is a natural partner of freshwater fish soups because the fish is somewhat bland and needs a little perking up.

The fish casserole from Hamburg is a rich dish, worthy of the prosperous harbor city from which it takes its name (recipe page 35, 4th column).

Fish patties with sweet-sour sauce

Büsumer Fischsuppe

Fish stew Büsum style

6–8 servings

4 medium onions, sliced
1 stalk celery, chopped
2 (1 lb.) packages frozen perch fillets, cut into serving size pieces
1 tablespoon salt
2 tablespoons margarine or butter
5 cups milk
½ cup sour cream
2 tablespoons chopped dill pickle
4 teaspoons horseradish
1 teaspoon parsley flakes
Fresh chopped dill

Place onions, celery, fish, salt and margarine in large heavy saucepan; add milk. Bring to a boil; reduce heat; simmer 15–20 minutes. Add sour cream, pickle, horseradish and parsley; stir to blend; heat. Garnish with dill.

Fischklopse in Specksauce

Fish patties with sweet-sour sauce

6 servings

1 cup croutons
¼ cup milk
1 pound cooked fish, ground
1 egg
1 tablespoon grated onion
½ teaspoon salt
1 cup fine bread crumbs
2 tablespoons margarine or butter
1 (10½ oz.) can cream of shrimp soup
½ cup milk
2 teaspoons vinegar

Soak croutons in milk until soft; drain well. Combine croutons, fish, egg, onion and salt; mix well. Add ¼–½ cup bread crumbs as needed to make a firm mixture. Shape into 2″ × 1″ patties. Roll in remaining bread crumbs.
Melt margarine in large skillet, brown patties in margarine.
Combine soup, milk and vinegar in saucepan; blend well. Heat. Serve sauce over patties.

Flunder, Hamburger Art

Whole flounder, Hamburg style

4 servings

- ½ *pound bacon, diced*
- 4 *flounder (about 12 oz. each) cleaned, pan-ready*
- 2 *teaspoons lemon juice*
- 1 *teaspoon salt*
- ¼ *cup flour*
- ¼ *cup margarine or butter*
- *Parsley sprigs*
- *Lemon wedges*

Fry diced bacon until crisp; drain on paper towels. Sprinkle each flounder with lemon juice and salt; coat with flour, shaking off excess. Melt margarine in large frying pan over moderately high heat. Fry fish slowly, about 5 minutes on each side, until golden brown. Arrange fish on platter, garnished with bacon pieces, parsley sprigs and lemon slices. Serve with potato sald.

Bremer Aalfrikassee

Eel fricassee

6 servings

- 1 *tablespoon beef extract*
- 3 *(1-pt.) bottles clam broth*
- 2 *pounds fresh eel, cleaned, skinned and cut into 1½″ pieces, or*
- 1½ *pounds red snapper or haddock fillet, cut into 1½″ × 1″ pieces*

Fish balls:

- 2 *onions, peeled and cut into 6 wedges each*
- ½ *pound haddock fillet*
- 2 *egg whites*
- ½ *cup top of milk*
- ½ *teaspoon salt*
- ⅛ *teaspoon pepper*

Sauce:

- 2 *tablespoons margarine or butter*
- 4 *tablespoons flour*
- 2 *cups poaching liquid*
- 2 *egg yolks*
- ½ *cup top of milk*
- ½ *cup dry white wine*
- 1 *(8 oz.) can sliced mushrooms, drained*
- ½ *pound frozen cooked, cleaned shrimp*
- 1 *(8 oz.) can cut asparagus pieces, drained*

Combine beef extract and clam broth in large, wide skillet or saucepan. Add eel or other fish pieces. Poach for 15 minutes or until fish flakes easily when tested with fork. Carefully remove fish. Keep warm. Reserve 2 cups liquid. Put onions and haddock fillet through finest blade of food grinder. Beat in egg whites, half-and-half and salt and pepper. Form into 1″ balls. Poach fish balls in hot, but not boiling water for about 10 minutes. Drain. Melt margarine in saucepan, stir in flour and reserved 2 cups broth; cook over medium heat, stirring constantly, until mixture thickens. Combine egg yolks with top of milk; add small amount of the hot mixture, stirring well. Return to saucepan, stirring briskly. Stir in wine, mushrooms, shrimp and asparagus. Add reserved poached fish and fish balls. Blend carefully. Serve hot with rice and cucumber salad.

Gedünste Fisch-Filets in Dillsauce

Poached fish fillets in dill sauce

4 servings

- 1½ *cups water*
- 1 *teaspoon salt*
- 1 *medium onion, sliced*
- 1 *bay leaf*
- 1 *(16 oz.) package frozen fish fillets, thawed*
- 2 *tablespoons margarine or butter*
- 2 *tablespoons flour*
- ½ *cup sour cream*
- 2 *tablespoons fresh dill, chopped*

In a large skillet, combine water, salt, onion, and bay leaf; bring to a boil. Turn down heat so that water is simmering. Carefully add fish fillets. Poach for 8–10 minutes or until fillets flake when tested with a fork. Gently remove fillets from pan; keep warm on serving platter. Strain fish broth and reserve 1 cup. In a small saucepan, melt margarine. Stir in flour; gradually add fish broth, stirring constantly. Cook until thickened. Remove from heat and stir in sour cream and dill. Serve sauce over fillets.

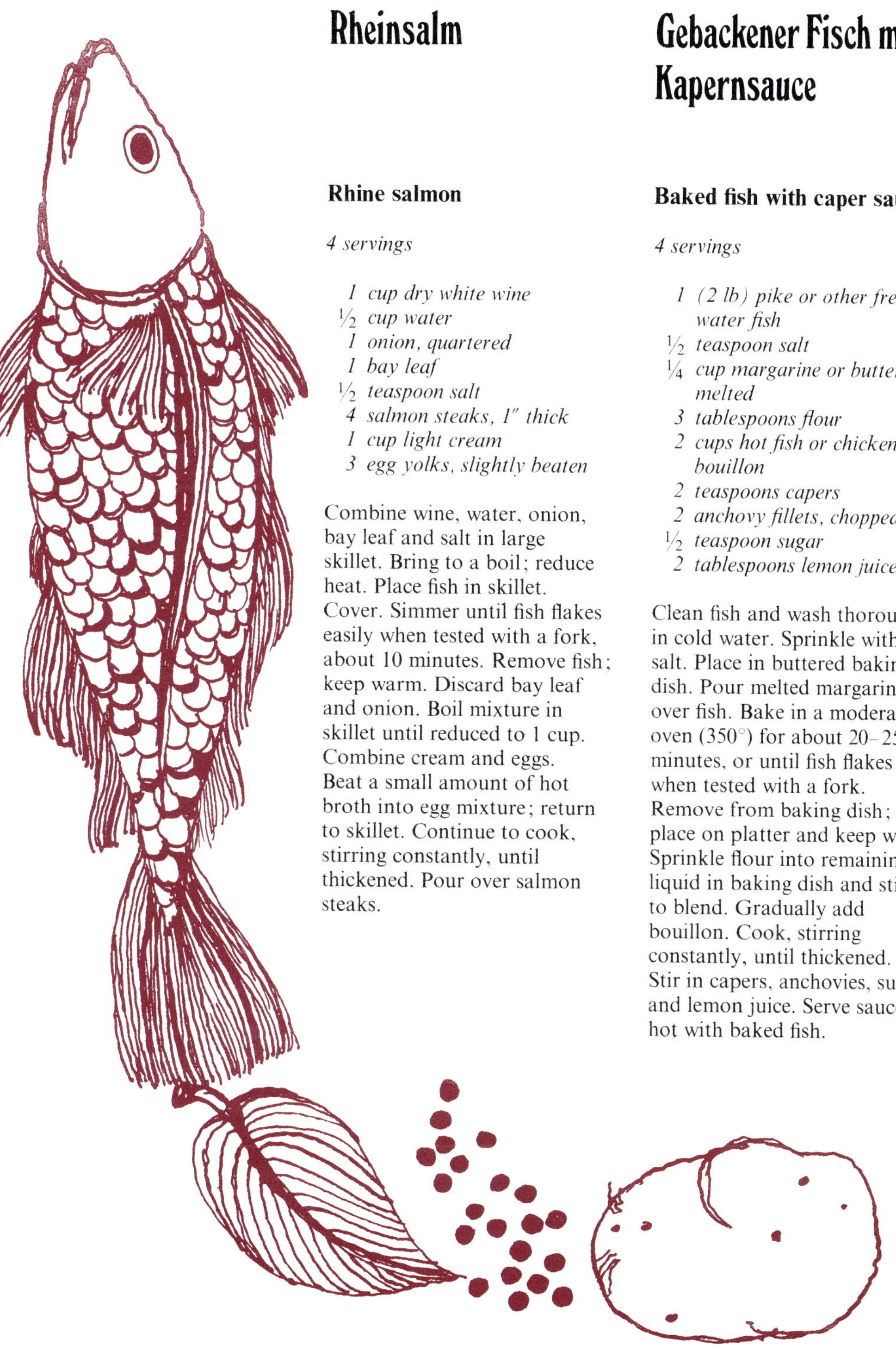

Rheinsalm

Rhine salmon

4 servings

- *1 cup dry white wine*
- *½ cup water*
- *1 onion, quartered*
- *1 bay leaf*
- *½ teaspoon salt*
- *4 salmon steaks, 1″ thick*
- *1 cup light cream*
- *3 egg yolks, slightly beaten*

Combine wine, water, onion, bay leaf and salt in large skillet. Bring to a boil; reduce heat. Place fish in skillet. Cover. Simmer until fish flakes easily when tested with a fork, about 10 minutes. Remove fish; keep warm. Discard bay leaf and onion. Boil mixture in skillet until reduced to 1 cup. Combine cream and eggs. Beat a small amount of hot broth into egg mixture; return to skillet. Continue to cook, stirring constantly, until thickened. Pour over salmon steaks.

Gebackener Fisch mit Kapernsauce

Baked fish with caper sauce

4 servings

- *1 (2 lb) pike or other fresh water fish*
- *½ teaspoon salt*
- *¼ cup margarine or butter, melted*
- *3 tablespoons flour*
- *2 cups hot fish or chicken bouillon*
- *2 teaspoons capers*
- *2 anchovy fillets, chopped*
- *½ teaspoon sugar*
- *2 tablespoons lemon juice*

Clean fish and wash thoroughly in cold water. Sprinkle with salt. Place in buttered baking dish. Pour melted margarine over fish. Bake in a moderate oven (350°) for about 20–25 minutes, or until fish flakes when tested with a fork. Remove from baking dish; place on platter and keep warm. Sprinkle flour into remaining liquid in baking dish and stir to blend. Gradually add bouillon. Cook, stirring constantly, until thickened. Stir in capers, anchovies, sugar, and lemon juice. Serve sauce hot with baked fish.

Friesischer Pfannfisch

Poached codfish

4–6 servings

- *2 pounds fresh codfish fillet or steak*
- *10 peppercorns, crushed*
- *1 bay leaf*
- *1 tablespoon chopped parsley*
- *2 cups water*
- *2 tablespoons margarine or butter*
- *2 tablespoons cornflour*
- *1½ tablespoons lemon juice*
- *Salt and pepper*
- *1½ pounds hot, cooked potatoes, cut into 1″ cubes*
- *Chopped parsley*

Place fish, peppercorns, bay leaf, parsley and water into a wide skillet or saucepan. Bring to the boiling point. (Do NOT allow to boil.) Poach until fish is tender, about 5–10 minutes. Carefully remove the fish to warm platter. Strain liquid, reserving 2 cups. Melt margarine in saucepan; blend in cornflour. Gradually add the reserved fish stock. Cook over medium heat, stirring constantly, until thickened, about 3–5 minutes. Stir in lemon juice. Season to taste with salt and pepper. Stir in potato cubes. Serve the sauce with the fish, or break the fish into approximately 1″ cubes and stir very gently into the sauce. Serve garnished with additional chopped parsley.

Trout from the numerous small brooks of Germany's mountains are considered a sort of national fish. The delicate taste is brought out best when the trout is poached and served with melted butter.

Gedünste Forelle

Poached trout

4 servings

- 2 *cups water*
- 1 *tablespoon parsley flakes*
- 1 *onion, quartered*
- 2 *bay leaves*
- 3 *cloves*
- 1 *teaspoon salt*
- 4 *trout, cleaned and pan-ready*
- ½ *cup melted margarine or butter*
- *Parsley sprigs*
- *Lemon wedge*

Combine water, parsley, onion, bay leaves, cloves and salt in large skillet. Bring to a boil; add fish. Reduce heat; cover; simmer 12–15 minutes or until fish flakes easily when tested with a fork. Carefully remove fish to serving dish; pour over melted margarine. Garnish with parsley sprigs and lemon wedges.

Trout and white wine (Hock or Moselle) are a celebrated combination in good German cuisine.

Gebackene Forelle Starnberger Art

Pan-fried trout Starnberg style

4 servings

- 4 *trout, cleaned and pan-ready*
- 2 *teaspoons Worcestershire sauce*
- 2 *teaspoons salt*
- 4 *tablespoons flour*
- 4 *tablespoons salad oil*
- 4 *tablespoons margarine or butter*
- 3 *shallots, finely minced or 1 small onion, finely chopped*
- 2 *tablespoons lemon juice*
- 1 *teaspoon parsley flakes*
- ½ *teaspoon dried tarragon*

Rub insides of fish with Worcestershire sauce, then with salt. Dredge fish with flour. Heat oil in large skillet. Fry fish in hot oil 3 minutes on each side. Remove fish; keep warm. Pour off oil. Melt margarine in skillet; stir in shallots, lemon juice, parsley, and tarragon; heat. Pour over fish.

Meat dishes

There is a droll German proverb that 'the most delicous vegetable in the world is meat' ...and another that 'in times of disaster sausages are eaten even without bread'.
Meat, as we can see, means quite a lot to the German diet, particularly in the form of 'Wurst' (sausage) which is the pillar of German cooking and is found in an almost endless variety of tastes: the light 'Weisswurst' from Munich, which is delicious with beer, the dark Thüringer Blutwurst (blood sausage), the hard Bierwurst, full-flavored Mettwurst, lightly sour Sülzle, spicy Kasseler or Berliner Leberwurst. They hang in the delicatessen in an appetizing and confusing array of colors and shapes: black, white, red and brown, hard and soft, long and short, thin and thick. At the wine feasts in Dürkheim and at the October beer festival in Munich, sausages are eaten by the million. For the great wine feast in Dürkheim alone, at least 200,000 liters of wine are poured out, and some 1000 oxen and 600 pigs disappear into the sausages.

Bremer Matrosenfleisch

Sailors' stew

6 servings

- *2 tablespoons salad oil*
- *1 pound beef, cut into 1″ cubes*
- *1 pound pork, cut into 1″ cubes*
- *2 medium onions, finely chopped*
- *2 carrots, chopped*
- *2 stalks celery, chopped*
- *1 teaspoon salt*
- *1/8 teaspoon black pepper*
- *1 bay leaf*
- *1 cup dry red wine*
- *1 teaspoon cornflour*
- *1/4 cup water*
- *2 teaspoons horseradish*

Heat oil in large Dutch oven. Brown meat on all sides.
Add vegetables, salt, pepper, bay leaf and wine. Bring to a boil. Cover. Reduce heat; simmer 45–50 minutes. Discard bay leaf.
Dissolve cornflour in water; add horseradish. Stir into beef mixture. Continue to cook, stirring constantly, until slightly thickened.

Rindsrouladen

Braised stuffed beef rolls

4 servings

- *8 very thin slices top side of beef*
- *1 medium onion, chopped*
- *1/4 pound bacon, diced*
- *1/4 cup flour*
- *1 teaspoon paprika*
- *1/2 teaspoon salt*
- *1/2 teaspoon pepper*
- *2 tablespoons salad oil*
- *1 carrot, sliced*
- *1 stalk celery, sliced*
- *1 small onion or 1 leek, sliced*
- *1/4 cup coarsely cut parsley*
- *1 cup hot water*
- *1 tablespoon cornflour*
- *2 tablespoons cold water*

Pound beef slices with mallet until very thin. Divide onion and bacon among the 8 beef slices, placing them across one end. Roll up with filling in center; secure rolls with toothpicks. Sprinkle all sides of rolls with flour, paprika, salt and pepper. In large skillet, brown in oil on all sides.
Add carrot, celery, onion or leek and parsley; add hot water. Cover and simmer until tender, about 1 1/2 to 2 hours, adding more water if needed. Remove rolls, remove toothpicks carefully and keep rolls warm. Strain and measure 1 cup liquid from skillet. Stir cornflour into cold water; add to measured meat juices. Cook over medium heat, stirring constantly, until thickened. Serve with beef rolls.

Schwäbischer Schlachtbraten

Swabian fillet of beef

6 servings

- *1 (3–3 1/2 lb.) beef tenderloin*
- *1 large onion, chopped*
- *1 stalk celery, chopped*
- *1 carrot, chopped*
- *4 tablespoons melted margarine or butter*
- *1 cup beef bouillon*
- *1 teaspoon flour*
- *2 tablespoons dry white wine*

Place meat on rack in roasting pan. Arrange vegetables around meat. Brush meat with melted butter. Insert meat thermometer into center of thickest part of meat. Roast in a very hot oven (450°), basting frequently, about 45–60 minutes or to 140° on thermometer. Remove meat; keep warm. Drain off fat, leaving brown bits in pan. Add bouillon to drippings in pan; scrape and stir until all brown bits are loosened.
Mash vegetables with fork. Strain into saucepan. Stir in flour and wine; heat thoroughly. Serve over meat.

Falscher Wildschweinbraten

Fake wild boar

6–8 servings

- 3 *pounds boneless rolled pork*
- 10 *juniper berries, crushed*
- 2 *teaspoons salt*
- 1 *teaspoon black pepper*
- 4 *tablespoons salad oil*
- ½ *cup dry red wine*
- ¼ *cup water*
- ½ *cup sour cream*
- 1 *tablespoon flour*
- 1 *tablespoon red currant jelly*

Rub meat with juniper berries, salt and pepper; let stand 15–20 minutes. Heat oil in Dutch oven; brown meat on all sides. Add wine and water; cover; simmer about 1 hour. Remove meat; keep warm. Drain off excess fat. Combine sour cream, flour and jelly; stir into drippings. Cook over low heat, stirring constantly until slightly thickened and smooth. Serve with meat.

Poached meatballs with lemon sauce, the traditional dish of the old East-Prussian city of Königsberg. You can make it even more piquant by sprinkling on a few capers.

Königsberger Klopse

Poached meatballs with lemon sauce

4 servings

1 pound ground beef
½ cup seasoned bread crumbs
1 egg
1 teaspoon grated lemon rind
1 cup water
2 beef bouillon cubes
1 tablespoon lemon juice
1 teaspoon cornflour
2 tablespoons cold water
1 egg yolk

Combine meat, bread crumbs, egg and lemon rind; mix lightly. Shape into 12 meatballs. Bring water to a boil in medium size saucepan; add bouillon cubes; stir until dissolved. Gently drop meatballs into simmering bouillon. Cook 8–10 minutes. Remove meatballs; keep warm. Add lemon juice to bouillon. Dissolve cornflour in cold water; stir into hot bouillon. Continue to cook stirring constantly, until slightly thickened. Add a small amount of hot bouillon mixture to egg yolk; beat well; stir into hot bouillon. Remove from heat and pour over meatballs.

With a German sauerbraten, you should always serve cooked, dried fruit.

Rheinischer Sauerbraten

Rhenish sauerbraten

6–8 servings

2 cups vinegar
2 cups water
4 onions, sliced
1 stalk celery, chopped
1 carrot, chopped
2 bay leaves
8 peppercorns, crushed
8 whole cloves
¼ teaspoon mustard seed
1 (4–5 lb.) rump roast of beef
1 teaspoon salt
¼ teaspoon pepper
¼ cup salad oil
4 tablespoons flour
½ cup seedless raisins
½ cup sour cream

Combine vinegar, water, onions, celery, carrot, bay leaves, peppercorns, cloves, and mustard seed in saucepan. Bring to a boil; cool. Place meat in large bowl. Pour marinade over meat. Place in refrigerator; marinate 2–3 days, turning several times. Remove meat from marinade; dry well. Sprinkle meat with salt and pepper. Heat oil in Dutch oven. Brown meat very well on all sides. Add 2 cups of the marinade; cover; simmer 2–3 hours or until meat is very tender. Remove meat; keep warm. Strain sauce; skim off fat; measure liquid. Add water or marinade to make 2 cups. Stir in flour. Return to pan. Cook over low heat, stirring and scraping browned bits, until thickened. Stir in raisins and sour cream; blend well. Serve with meat.

Bayerischer Jägertopf

Hunter's casserole

4 servings

1½ pounds beef for stew
½ teaspoon salt
⅛ teaspoon black pepper
2 large onions, chopped
1 (6 oz.) can sliced mushrooms, drained
½ cup dry red wine
1 cup beef bouillon
3 carrots, sliced
3 medium potatoes, sliced

Sprinkle meat with salt and pepper. Heat oil in heavy saucepot. Brown meat well in hot oil. Add onions and mushrooms; cook until onions are transparent. Add wine; cover; simmer 30 minutes. Add bouillon; continue to simmer 30 minutes. Add carrots and potatoes; stir well. Cook, covered, 20–25 minutes or until vegetables are tender.

Schmorbraten mit saurer Sahnensauce

Pot roast with sour cream gravy

6–8 servings

2 tablespoons salad oil
1 (4–5 lb.) sirloin of beef
1 medium onion, sliced
1 cup dry red wine
1 cup water
2 tablespoons flour
¼ cup cold water
1 teaspoon salt
¼ teaspoon black pepper
½ cup sour cream

Heat oil in Dutch oven; brown meat on all sides. Add onion, wine, and water. Cover and simmer gently for 3–4 hours or until tender. Remove meat and keep warm. Drain off all but 1½ cups liquid. Stir flour into cold water until blended; slowly stir into liquid in pan. Add salt and pepper. Cook, stirring, over low heat until thickened. Slowly blend in sour cream. Serve gravy with sliced pot roast.

Geschmorte Schweinerippen

Smothered pork chops

4 servings

4 pork chops, about ¾″ thick
1 teaspoon salt
1 teaspoon dry mustard
1 tablespoon lemon juice
4 tablespoons margarine or butter
1 medium onion, chopped
1 (1 lb.) can whole, peeled tomatoes

Rub chops on both sides with salt, mustard and lemon juice; let stand for 30 minutes. Melt margarine in skillet; brown chops on both sides. Add onions; let cook a few minutes over medium heat until transparent. Add tomatoes with liquid. Cover and simmer until tender, about 20–30 minutes. If sauce becomes too thick or starts to separate, add a few tablespoons hot water. Serve immediately.

Kasseler Rippchen mit Sauerkraut

Smoked pork tenderloin with sauerkraut

4–6 servings

1 (2–3 lb.) smoked pork tenderloin
1 (16 oz.) can sauerkraut
1 tablespoon minced onion
1 teaspoon caraway seed

Prepare the tenderloin according to directions on package. Cut into ½″ slices. Mix together sauerkraut, onion, and caraway seed. Spread sauerkraut mixture over the bottom of a large casserole dish. Top with tenderloin slices. Bake in a moderate oven (350°) for 15–20 minutes or until sauerkraut is heated.

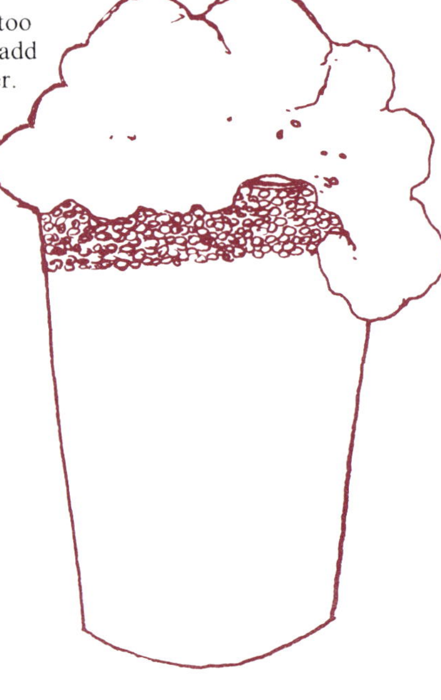

Schlesischer Schwärtelbraten

Silesian fresh ham

8 servings

- *1 fresh ham (5–6 lb.)*
- *1 teaspoon salt*
- *½ teaspoon black pepper*
- *1 teaspoon caraway seed*
- *1 cup boiling water*
- *1 medium onion, sliced*
- *1 tablespoon cornflour*
- *¼ cup cold water*
- *½ cup sour cream (optional)*

Rub meat with salt, pepper, and caraway seed. Place on rack in roasting pan. Pour water in bottom of roasting pan; add onions. Roast in moderate oven (350°) for 3–3½ hours or until a meat thermometer reaches 185°. Remove from pan and keep warm. Pour off all but 3 tablespoons of fat. Remove onions. Stir to loosen drippings from pan, adding water as necessary to increase liquid to 1 cup. Mix cornflour with cold water. Add to gravy. Cook over low heat, stirring constantly, until thickened. If desired, stir in sour cream. Slice meat and serve with gravy.

Bayerische Haxen

Bavarian veal or pork roast

6 servings

- *1 (4 lb.) rump of veal or 1 (3 lb.) boneless pork shoulder roll*
- *1 teaspoon salt*
- *½ cup boiling water*
- *1 large onion, thinly sliced*
- *1 carrot, chopped*
- *3 peppercorns, crushed*
- *½ teaspoon caraway seed*

Place meat in roasting pan. Sprinkle with salt. Pour boiling water into pan. Add vegetables, peppercorns and caraway seed. Roast in a moderate oven (350°) until meat tests done on a meat thermometer, veal 170°; pork 185°, about 1 hour, 45 minutes. Baste with pan juices during roasting, adding more water if needed.

It is said that this typical East German dish owes its name 'Himmelreich' meaning Kingdom of Heaven, to the dried fruit that accompanies it. The fruit grows high up in the trees.

Schlesisches Himmelreich

Silesian pork and dried fruit

4–6 servings

- *1 tablespoon flour*
- *2 pounds boneless rolled pork*
- *1 cup dried apricots*
- *1 cup dried pitted prunes*
- *¼ cup granulated brown sugar*
- *½ cup dry white wine*

Dust the inside of a cooking bag with flour. Place meat and fruit in cooking bag; sprinkle with brown sugar. Pour wine over all. Tie bag securely. Puncture 4 small holes about 4″ apart in top of bag. Place bag in shallow roasting pan. Cook in a slow oven (325°) 1½ hours. Place meat on serving platter; arrange fruit around meat.

Kasseler Rippenspeer

Smoked loin of pork

6–8 servings

- 1 (4–5 lb.) smoked loin of pork
- ¼ teaspoon black pepper
- 1 medium onion, sliced
- 1 cup hot water
- 1 cup dry red wine
- Braised sauerkraut page 69

Place meat in shallow roasting pan; sprinkle with pepper; add onion. Pour hot water over meat. Roast in a hot oven (400°) 30 minutes. Pour half the wine over meat. Continue to roast, basting frequently with remaining wine, about 30 minutes or until meat is well browned. Serve with braised sauerkraut.

Smoked loin of pork. That delicious cooking smell that fills German houses in the wintertime is the unmistakable evidence of sauerkraut being prepared with smoked pork.

Creamed veal cutlets (recipe page 50, 2nd column).

Westfälische Hammelkeule

Westphalian leg of lamb

4–6 servings

- *1 small onion, chopped*
- *1 carrot, chopped*
- *1 tablespoon chopped parsley*
- *2 tablespoons margarine or butter*
- *1 bay leaf*
- *1 (8 oz.) container plain yogurt or*
- *1 cup buttermilk*
- *1 tablespoon flour*
- *½ leg of lamb (about 3½ lbs.)*
- *1 teaspoon salt*
- *⅛ teaspoon pepper*
- *1 tablespoon cornflour*
- *2 tablespoons cold water*

Sauté onion, carrot and parsley in margarine until onion is transparent. Add bay leaf and yogurt. Sprinkle flour in cooking bag large enough to contain the lamb. Place half of the yogurt mixture in the bag. Sprinkle lamb with salt and pepper. Place in bag on the yogurt mixture. Cover lamb with remaining mixture. Seal bag with twist tie. Puncture bag in 3 or 4 places with a 2-tined fork. Insert meat thermometer into the thickest part of the meat. Roast in a moderate oven (350°) until lamb registers 165° for medium or 180° for well-done. Carefully strain liquid from bag. Measure and make up to 1 cup with water, if necessary. Stir cornflour into cold water. Add to liquid; cook over medium heat until thickened, stirring constantly. Taste, season with salt and pepper. Serve sauce with sliced lamb.

Rahmschnitzel mit Spätzle

Creamed veal cutlets with spatzle

4 servings

- *1 pound (4) veal cutlets*
- *½ teaspoon salt*
- *⅛ teaspoon black pepper*
- *4 tablespoons margarine or butter*
- *2 tablespoons chopped chives*
- *1 teaspoon parsley flakes*
- *½ cup dry white wine*
- *1 tablespoon flour*
- *½ cup sour cream*
- *1 recipe spatzle page 69 or hot cooked noodles*

Sprinkle cutlets with salt and pepper. Melt margarine in large skillet. Brown cutlets in margarine. Add chives, parsley and wine. Cover. Simmer 20–25 minutes. Remove cutlets; keep warm. Blend in flour. Cook, stirring constantly, until slightly thickened. Stir in sour cream; heat thoroughly pour over veal. Serve with spatzle or noodles.

Weimarer Ochsenzunge

Tongue with raisin sauce

8 servings

- *1 pre-cooked beef tongue (3–4 lbs.)*
- *Water to cover*
- *1 onion, sliced*
- *1 celery stalk*
- *1 sprig of parsley*
- *2 tablespoons margarine or butter*
- *2 tablespoons flour*
- *½ teaspoon salt*
- *2 tablespoons vinegar*
- *2 tablespoons sugar*
- *⅔ cup raisins*

Place tongue in deep saucepan with any juices packed with tongue; add water to cover. Add onion, celery, and parsley. Heat thoroughly; remove tongue and keep warm. Strain liquid and reserve 1½ cups. Melt margarine in saucepan; stir in flour and salt; slowly add the reserved cooking fluid. Stir until smooth and thickened; stir in vinegar, sugar, and raisins. Continue to cook until well heated. Serve with sliced tongue.

Nieren Stuttgarter Art

Kidneys Stuttgart style

4 servings

- *1½ pounds beef kidneys*
- *2 tablespoons flour*
- *1 teaspoon salt*
- *¼ teaspoon black pepper*
- *2 medium onions, sliced*
- *¼ cup margarine or butter*
- *1 cup beef bouillon*
- *2 tablespoons lemon juice*
- *¼ cup chopped parsley*
- *⅓ cup cream or evaporated milk*
- *2 tablespoons white wine (optional)*
- *1 teaspoon paprika*
- *1 tablespoon chopped chives*

Soak kidneys in lightly salted water for about 1–2 hours. Slice and remove white membranes. Dry well. Dredge with flour seasoned with salt and pepper. Melt margarine in skillet and sauté onions until golden. Remove from pan. Sauté kidney slices until lightly browned. Add onions, bouillon, lemon juice, and parsley. Stir in cream or evaporated milk, and wine. Simmer for 5 minutes. Sprinkle with paprika and chives. Serve with rice.

Berliner Leber

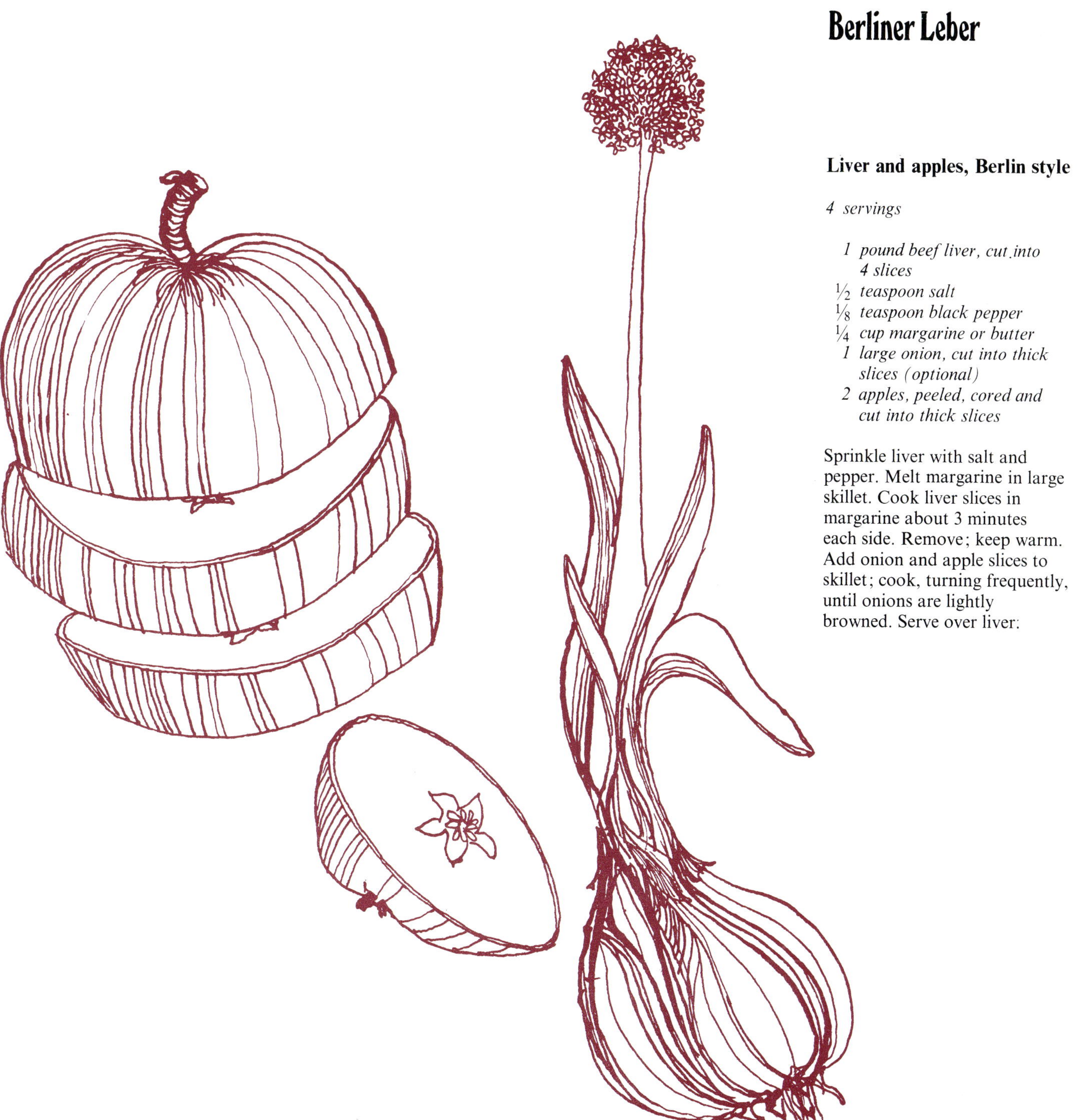

Liver and apples, Berlin style

4 servings

1 pound beef liver, cut into 4 slices
½ teaspoon salt
⅛ teaspoon black pepper
¼ cup margarine or butter
1 large onion, cut into thick slices (optional)
2 apples, peeled, cored and cut into thick slices

Sprinkle liver with salt and pepper. Melt margarine in large skillet. Cook liver slices in margarine about 3 minutes each side. Remove; keep warm. Add onion and apple slices to skillet; cook, turning frequently, until onions are lightly browned. Serve over liver.

Geschnetzelte Leber

Liver with mushrooms and white wine

4 servings

- *4 slices bacon, diced*
- *1/4 cup finely chopped onion*
- *1 (6 oz.) package frozen sliced mushrooms*
- *1 pound sliced baby beef liver, about 4 slices*
- *1 tablespoon flour*
- *1/2 teaspoon salt*
- *Dash black pepper*
- *1/2 cup dry white wine*
- *1 cup top of milk or light cream*
- *1 tablespoon chopped parsley*

In large frying pan over moderate heat, fry bacon until crisp. Remove bacon pieces, drain and reserve. Add chopped onion and mushrooms to bacon fat in pan. Cook over medium heat until onions are transparent. Remove skins and tubes from liver; cut into 1/4″ × 1/2″ × 2″ strips. Add to hot fat and toss to brown, 3–4 minutes. Sprinkle flour, salt and pepper over liver. Stir to blend. Stir in wine, then top of milk. Heat to a boil; reduce heat and simmer 4–5 minutes. Serve garnished with parsley and reserved bacon pieces. Serve with rice or spatzle.

Gefüllte Kalbsbrust

Stuffed breast of veal

4–6 servings

- *1 (3 1/2 lb.) breast of veal with pocket for stuffing*
- *1/2 teaspoon salt*
- *1/8 teaspoon black pepper*
- *3/4 cup finely chopped onion*
- *2 tablespoons chopped parsley*
- *4 slices day old bread, cubed*
- *2 tablespoons top of milk*
- *2 tablespoons salad oil*
- *2 eggs*
- *1/2 teaspoon paprika*
- *1/2 teaspoon salt*
- *Dash black pepper*
- *1/4 cup margarine or butter*
- *1/2 cup water*
- *1 tablespoon cornflour*
- *1/4 cup currant jelly*
- *1 teaspoon lemon juice*

Sprinkle inside pocket and outside of veal with salt and pepper. Mix together onion, parsley, bread cubes, top of milk, oil, eggs, paprika, salt and pepper. Fill pocket with bread mixture; skewer shut. Melt margarine in Dutch oven. Place meat in margarine; add water. Cover. Cook over medium heat until veal is tender when pierced with a fork, about 1 1/2 hours. Turn meat once after 45 minutes. Remove veal; keep warm. Measure any liquid in pan; add water to make 1 cup. Stir in cornflour; return to pan. Cook over medium heat, stirring and scraping up browned bits, until thickened. Add jelly and lemon juice; stir until jelly is dissolved. Serve with veal.

A typical German Sunday dish: stuffed breast of veal, thickly sliced, with a delicious, slightly sour sauce of currant jelly and lemon juice.

Liver with mushrooms and white wine

Liver and apples, Berlin style
(recipe page 51, 4th column)

Bratwurst

Braised sausage

4 servings

- $1\frac{1}{2}$ *pounds sausages*
- $\frac{1}{4}$ *cup fine dry bread crumbs*
- 4 *tablespoons margarine or butter*
- $\frac{1}{2}$ *cup chopped onion*
- 1 *tablespoon flour*
- 1 *cup water*
- 1 *tablespoon tomato sauce*
- $\frac{1}{4}$ *teaspoon salt*
- $\frac{1}{4}$ *teaspoon thyme*

Place sausages in large skillet, in one layer; just cover with hot water. Simmer 1–2 minutes until sausages are no longer pink. (Be sure sausages are cooked to center). Discard water. Drain on paper towels. Roll sausages in bread crumbs, coating well. Heat margarine in same skillet until quite hot. Place sausages in skillet; prick with a sharp-tined fork. Brown on all sides over moderate heat. Remove from pan and keep warm. Cook onion in fat remaining in pan over low heat until onion is transparent. Stir in flour, gradually add water and cook over medium heat, stirring frequently, until thickened, about 1 minute. Stir in tomato sauce. Season with salt to taste. Stir in thyme Serve gravy over sausages with mashed potatoes.

Poultry and game dishes

Bremer Kükenragout

Chicken ragout

8 servings

- *8 frying chicken parts (legs, breasts or both)*
- *1 teaspoon salt*
- *¼ cup margarine or butter*
- *2 cups chicken bouillon or hot water*
- *2 tablespoons flour*
- *1 pound frozen, cooked, shelled and deveined shrimp*
- *1 (10 oz.) package frozen peas with sliced mushrooms*
- *1 (8½ oz.) can cut asparagus pieces, drained*
- *¼ cup sour cream*
- *1 tablespoon lemon juice*

Sprinkle chicken parts with salt. Melt margarine in frying pan; brown chicken pieces on all sides. Pour in bouillon, cover, and simmer over moderate heat about 15 minutes, until chicken is tender. Remove chicken to warm platter. Pour off bouillon and measure 1½ cups. (Any additional bouillon may be used for soups or in other recipes). In a saucepan, stir a small amount of the bouillon into the flour. Add remaining bouillon gradually. Cook over medium heat, stirring contantly, until thickened. Add frozen shrimp, cover and simmer until shrimp are thawed. Stir in peas and mushrooms, sour cream and asparagus. Heat gently, but do not allow to boil. Taste. If desired, add lemon juice. Serve hot over chicken pieces with mashed potatoes and a green salad.

Böhmisches Huhn

Chicken à la Bohème

3–4 servings

- *1 (2–3 lb.) roasting chicken*
- *½ teaspoon salt*
- *4 ounces vermicelli spaghetti, cooked*
- *¼ cup chopped parsley*
- *¼ cup grated cheese*
- *1 egg*
- *1 tablespoon margarine or butter*
- *2 cups chicken bouillon*

Wash and dry chicken; sprinkle salt in cavity. Mix cooked spaghetti, parsley, cheese, and egg; stuff chicken with mixture Rub margarine on chicken. Place in roasting pan on rack. Roast in (350°) oven for about 1½ hours or until chicken is done when tested. Remove chicken from pan. Cut in half lengthwise; place vermicelli stuffing on platter and place chicken halves on top. Pour bouillon into roasting pan and stir to combine with pan juices; serve as gravy.

Huhn mit Gemüse und Kräuter

Chicken poached with vegetables and herbs

8 servings

- *2 (2–3 lb.) frying chickens cut into serving pieces*
- *1 tablespoon flour*
- *1 teaspoon salt*
- *⅛ teaspoon pepper*
- *¼ pound bacon, diced*
- *1 medium onion, chopped*
- *1 medium carrot, chopped*
- *¼ cup chopped parsley*
- *1 medium sized tart apple, cored and chopped or*
- *¼ cup canned apple slices, chopped*
- *6 peppercorns*
- *1 bay leaf*
- *½ teaspoon whole dried thyme*
- *½ cup dry white wine*
- *Hot cooked noodles*

Sprinkle flour in cooking bag large enough to contain chicken pieces comfortably. Sprinkle chicken with salt and pepper. Cook diced bacon in large skillet until crisp. Add chopped vegetables and apple; cook over medium heat until transparent. Add peppercorns, bay leaf and thyme. Spread mixture in cooking bag in pan with 2″ sides. Place chicken pieces on vegetables; add wine. Close bag with twist tie; puncture bag with sharp-tined fork 3 or 4 times. Place pan with bag in moderately slow oven (325°) until chicken is tender and slightly browned, about 1 hour. Serve with hot buttered noodles.

Hähnchen Berliner Art

Hens, Berlin style

4 servings

- *4 (1¼ lb.) frozen hens, thawed*
- *1 (6 oz.) package rice and wild rice, prepared according to package directions*
- *1 small onion, chopped*
- *1 stalk celery, finely chopped*
- *½ cup seedless grapes, halved*
- *½ cup slivered almonds*
- *½ teaspoon salt*
- *½ teaspoon thyme*
- *¼ cup melted margarine or butter*

Wash and dry hens. Combine rice, onion, celery, grapes, almonds, salt and thyme; mix well. Fill neck and body cavities lightly with stuffing; skewer openings shut. Place hens in large shallow roasting pan; brush with melted margarine. Roast hens in a hot oven (400°) about 1 hour or until well browned and drumstick twists easily out of thigh joint, basting several times with margarine.

Gebratene Hähnchen

Roast hens

4 servings

- *4 (1 lb.) frozen hens, thawed*
- *1 teaspoon salt*
- *¼ teaspoon black pepper*
- *4 slices bacon, diced*
- *2 slices day-old bread*
- *⅓ cup milk*
- *1 tablespoon chopped parsley*
- *5 tablespoons margarine or butter*
- *1 cup beef bouillon*
- *1 tablespoon flour*
- *½ cup sour cream*

Wash and dry hens. Rub inside cavities with salt and pepper. In a skillet, cook bacon until crisp. Brown the livers of the hens; chop into small pieces. Soften bread in milk and squeeze out. Add bacon, chopped livers, and parsley. Stuff hens with mixture. Melt margarine in roasting pan and brown each hen. Roast in moderate oven (350°) for 1–1½ hours or until hens are cooked. Remove hens and keep warm. Pour bouillon into roasting pan and stir over direct heat to loosen drippings. Stir in flour. Cook until slightly thickened. Stir in sour cream. Serve gravy with roast hens.

Berlin style chicken fricassee

Berliner Hühnerfrikassee

Berlin style chicken fricassee

6 servings

- *2 (8 oz.) cans chicken gravy*
- *4 tablespoons dry white wine*
- *1 tablespoon lemon juice*
- *2 cups cubed, cooked chicken*
- *1 cup diced ham*
- *6 sausages, cooked and sliced*
- *1 (3 oz.) can sliced mushrooms, drained*
- *1 tablespoon capers*
- *1 (8½ oz.) can asparagus pieces, drained*
- *½ cup sour cream*
- *Hot cooked rice*

Combine gravy, wine and lemon juice in saucepan; blend well. Stir in chicken, ham, sausages and mushrooms. Heat, stirring constantly. Add capers and asparagus spears; heat. Stir in sour cream until well blended. Serve over rice.

Festlicher Putenbraten

Roast stuffed turkey

8–10 servings

- *1 tablespoon margarine or butter*
- *1 large onion, chopped*
- *1 apple, peeled, cored and chopped*
- *1 pound ground pork*
- *½ pound sausage meat*
- *8 dried apricots, halved*
- *8 prunes, pitted and halved*
- *1 (8 oz.) package stuffing mix*
- *1 cup apple juice or water*
- *1 (10–12 lb.) turkey*
- *1 onion, quartered*
- *1 stalk celery, chopped*
- *2 teaspoons salt*
- *4 tablespoons flour*

Melt margarine in large skillet; sauté onion and apple in margarine until onion is transparent. Add meat; cook until lightly browned, stirring constantly. Add fruit, stuffing mix and juice; blend lightly. Remove giblets from turkey; place in 1 quart saucepan with onion, celery and 1 teaspoon salt. Cover with water. Simmer, covered, about 1–1½ hours. Strain; reserve stock. Rub neck and body cavities of turkey lightly with remaining teaspoon salt. Stuff neck and body cavities lightly with stuffing; skewer openings shut. Place turkey, breast side up, on rack in shallow roasting pan. Insert meat thermometer in thigh muscle. Place a loose tent of foil over bird (remove last 30 minutes). Roast in a slow oven (325°) about 2½–3 hours or until thermometer reads 185°. Move drumstick up and down; if it moves easily, bird is done. Place bird on warm platter. Drain off fat. Stir flour into 2 cups stock; add to drippings. Cook over medium heat, stirring constantly, until thickened.

Pommeranian roast goose. There are always numbers of geese wobbling about the farmyards of the large old Pommeranian farms of East Germany. Goose tastes best if prepared in November or December, and it should always be cooked in its own fat.

Roast duckling with apples *(recipe page 59, 3rd column)*

Pommerscher Gänsebraten

The goose is the favorite German fowl. In the small villages and towns of the countryside they make a charming and amusing sight as they walk in long lines along the streets. Geese are anything but stupid, though they are often maligned. In ancient times, the loud warning given by a gaggle of alert geese is said to have prevented the treacherous overthrow of the Roman capitol. A Scottish whisky distillery still uses geese to watch over its precious stocks because these sensitive birds seem to do the job far better than dogs. During the Middle Ages geese were trained to rotate the large roasting spits used for preparing wild pigs: the geese held one end of the spit in their beaks and turned it by thrusting their necks in and out. The idea that geese are stupid is obviously an injustice perpetuated by the ignorant.

A goose roasted in the German way, with apples, prunes and herbs, is a dish fit for a king and is one of the very favorite Christmas dinners in Germany.

Pommeranian roast goose

4–6 servings

1 (8–9 lb.) goose
1 onion, chopped
1 tablespoon salt
1½ cups pitted prunes, halved
4 tart apples, peeled, cored and quartered
1 cup coarse rye bread crumbs
2 tablespoons sugar
4 tablespoons flour

Wash and dry goose. Remove giblets; place in 1 quart saucepan with onion and 1 teaspoon salt. Cover with water. Simmer, partially covered, about 1–1½ hours. Strain; reserve stock. Sprinkle goose inside and out with salt. Combine prunes, apples, rye bread and sugar; fill cavity of bird. Skewer openings together. Place on rack in shallow roasting pan, breast side down. Roast in a hot oven (400°) 45 minutes. Drain fat from roasting pan. Reduce oven temperature to 325°; roast until tender when pierced with a fork, and juices are light yellow, not pink, about 1 hour. Drain fat from pan. Turn goose breast side up; brown until golden, about 30 minutes. Remove; keep warm. Skim off remaining fat. Stir flour into 2 cups stock; add to drippings in pan. Cook over medium heat, stirring and scraping browned bits, until thickened. Serve with goose.

Thüringer Gans

Thuringian roast goose

4–6 servings

- *1 (8–9 lb.) goose, fresh or frozen*
- *1 tablespoon salt*
- *1 teaspoon dried marjoram*
- *2 medium onions, peeled*
- *1 stalk celery, broken into 3–4 pieces*
- *Salt*
- *Pepper*
- *6 cloves*
- *2 apples, well washed*
- *1 cup chicken or goose stock or water*
- *1 cup orange juice*
- *2 tablespoons cornflour*
- *¼ cup cold water*

Thaw goose, if frozen. Remove giblets; place in 1-qt. saucepan with one of the onions, celery pieces, salt and pepper. Cover with water. Simmer, partially covered, for about 1–1½ hours. Strain; reserve stock. Meanwhile, wash and dry goose; sprinkle inside and out with salt. Sprinkle marjoram inside, stick cloves in second onion and place in cavity with the apples. Skewer openings together. Place goose on a rack in a large roasting pan, breast side down. Roast in a hot oven (400°) for 45 minutes. Drain fat from roasting pan. Reduce oven temperature to 325° and roast until tender when pierced with a fork and juices are light yellow, not pink, about 1 hour. Drain fat from pan. Turn goose breast side up on rack; brown in oven until golden, about 30 minutes. Remove to a warm platter. Skim off remaining fat. Add stock or water and orange juice to pan juices. Mix cornflour and cold water, add to pan. Cook over medium heat, stirring constantly, until gravy is thickened.

Vierländer Mastente

Roast duckling with apples

4–6 servings

- *1 (4–5 lb.) frozen duckling thawed*
- *1 teaspoon salt*
- *¼ teaspoon black pepper*
- *4 apples, thinly sliced and peeled*
- *2–3 slices day-old bread, cubed*
- *½ teaspoon poultry seasoning*
- *¼ cup blackberry brandy (or orange juice)*
- *1 onion, sliced*

Thoroughly wash duck. Sprinkle inside cavity with salt and pepper. Mix apple slices, bread cubes, poultry seasoning and brandy. Stuff duck with mixture. Place on rack in roasting pan. Prick breast with fork. Place onion in pan around duck. Roast, uncovered, at (325°) for 2½–3 hours. Pour off fat as it accumulates. Baste occasionally with pan drippings. Serve with baked stuffed apples, if desired.

Ente, Berliner Art

Berlin style duckling

4 servings

- *1 frozen duckling (about 5 pounds), thawed*
- *1½ teaspoons salt*
- *¼ teaspoon black pepper*
- *½ teaspoon powdered marjoram*
- *4 tart apples, peeled, cored and quartered*
- *¾ cup hot water*
- *1 tablespoon cornflour*
- *2 tablespoons cold water*

Wash and dry thawed duckling. Sprinkle inside and out with salt and pepper. Sprinkle marjoram inside, place apples in cavity and skewer shut. Pour water into roasting pan. Place duckling breast side down in pan. Roast in moderate oven (350°) for about 40 minutes. Pour off fat. Baste frequently with pan juices. Turn duck over, cook another 50–60 minutes or until thigh is tender when pierced with a fork and juices are yellow, not pink. Remove duck to a warm platter. Pour off fat. Measure drippings, make up to 1 cup with water or stock. Stir cornflour into cold water, add to pan juices. Cook over medium heat, stirring constantly, until thickened. Serve with carved duckling.

Hasenpfeffer

Rabbit in wine gravy

4 servings

1 (2½–3 lb.) rabbit, cut up
2 cups red wine
1 cup water
¼ cup vinegar
1 onion, sliced
1 tablespoon sugar
2 tablespoons salt
1 teaspoon whole cloves
¼ teaspoon black pepper
3 bay leaves
½ cup flour
¼ cup salad oil

Place rabbit in large bowl. Combine wine, water, vinegar, onion, sugar, salt, cloves, pepper and bay leaves; pour over meat. Place in refrigerator; marinate 12–24 hours. Remove rabbit; dry well. Dredge rabbit with flour; save remaining flour. Heat oil in Dutch oven. Brown rabbit in hot oil. Strain marinade; add 2½ cups to rabbit. Cover; simmer 1 hour or until meat is tender. Remove rabbit; keep warm. If a thicker sauce is desired, stir in remaining flour. Cook over medium heat, stirring constantly, until sauce is thickened. Serve over meat.

Fasan, Badische Art

Pheasant, Baden style

4 servings

1 (2¼–3 lb.) pheasant
1½ teaspoons salt
¼ cup melted margarine or butter
1 tablespoon brandy
1 teaspoon grated lemon rind
¼ teaspoon powdered thyme
1½ cups water
1 tablespoon flour

Wash pheasant; dry well. Sprinkle ½ teaspoon salt over insides of bird. Place bird on rack in shallow roasting pan. Combine margarine, brandy, rind, ½ teaspoon salt and thyme; brush bird generously. Roast in a moderately hot oven (375°) about 55 minutes, basting bird frequently with margarine mixture. Combine giblets, water and remaining salt in saucepan; cook until tender. Remove giblets. Strain broth; save. Remove bird; skim off fat. Stir flour into 1 cup broth; return to pan. Cook over low heat, stirring constantly, until thickened. Serve with pheasant.

Braunschweiger Geflügelklein

Giblet and pork stew

4 servings

3 cloves
1 medium onion, peeled
1½ pounds chicken giblets (hearts, livers, gizzards, necks and wings)
1 quart water
½ teaspoon salt
1 small bay leaf
½ pound sausage meat
¼ cup margarine or butter
3 tablespoons flour
1 cup milk
1 teaspoon grated lemon rind
1 (8½ oz.) can cut asparagus pieces, drained
1 (6 oz.) can sliced mushrooms, drained

Stick cloves into onion. Wash and trim giblets. Place onion, giblets, water, salt and bay leaf into a saucepan. Simmer, uncovered, until giblets are tender, about 1 hour. Drain, reserving 1 cup liquid. Cut giblets and pieces of chicken meat into 1″ pieces. Shape sausage meat into 1″ balls. In frying pan, over medium heat, brown sausage balls on all sides. Melt margarine in saucepan. Stir in flour, gradually add the 1 cup reserved liquid and milk, stirring constantly, until sauce is thickened, about 2–3 minutes. Stir in lemon rind, giblets, sausage balls, asparagus and mushrooms. Cook over low heat until hot. Do not boil. Serve with rice and peas.

Schwäbische Kaninchenpastete

Rabbit pate en croûte

8 servings

1 (2–2½ lb.) package frozen rabbit, thawed and boned
4 tablespoons margarine or butter
1 onion, peeled and cut into 6 wedges
1 clove garlic, crushed (if desired)
½ cup chopped parsley
1 (6 oz.) can sliced mushrooms, drained
¼ teaspoon thyme
½ cup dry white wine
1 (10 oz.) package frozen puff pastry
1 egg, beaten lightly

Heat margarine in skillet. Over medium heat, brown rabbit meat on all sides. Put meat and onion through food grinder, using fine blade. Combine with garlic, parsley, mushrooms, thyme, wine and the margarine remaining in skillet. Blend well. Roll out the thawed pastry to ⅛″ thick. Carefully line a 9″ × 5″ × 3″ loaf pan with the pastry; moisten edges slightly and press together firmly. Fill the pastry-lined pan with the rabbit mixture. Fold pastry over top and seal tightly. With point of knife, make three ½″ holes in top for steam vents. Brush beaten egg over surface. Bake in moderate oven (350°) about 1 hour. Cool and turn out of pan. Serve warm or cool.

Schlesischer Hasenbraten

Silesian roast hare

4–6 servings

- *1 (2½–3 lb.) package frozen rabbit parts, thawed*
- *4 slices bacon, diced*
- *1 teaspoon salt*
- *¼ teaspoon black pepper*
- *¼ teaspoon nutmeg*
- *¼ teaspoon thyme*
- *¼ cup flour*
- *2 slices pimiento, diced*
- *1 cup water*
- *½ cup sour cream*

Wash and dry pieces of rabbit. Brown diced bacon; drain on paper towels. Reserve bacon drippings. Place salt, pepper, nutmeg, thyme, and flour in a paper bag. Shake rabbit parts in bag until fully coated with seasoned flour. Brown in bacon drippings. Add pimiento and cook until all parts are tender. Remove rabbit and keep warm. Pour water into pan and heat, scraping pan to blend. Stir in sour cream. Add crisp pieces of bacon. Serve rabbit with hot gravy.

Mixed meat and vegetables stew
(recipe page 64, 1st column)

Frankfurt noodle casserole. When Germans invite friends out for cocktails, they always serve a warm casserole just before the guests leave. It gives them the courage to face the long trip home.

Frankfurter Nudelpfanne

Frankfurt noodle casserole

6 servings

- 1 *(8 oz.) package noodles, cooked and drained*
- 1 *(10 oz.) package frozen peas, thawed*
- 4 *tablespoons margarine or butter*
- 1 *(10 oz.) package frozen spinach, cooked and drained*
- 1 *pound frankfurters, sliced*
- 1 *(10½ oz.) can cream of mushroom soup*
- ½ *cup sour cream*
- ½ *cup milk*
- 4 *slices bacon, cooked and crumbled*

Combine noodles, 1½ cups peas, and margarine; mix lightly. Place spinach in bottom of buttered 2½ qt. casserole. Spread noodle mixture over spinach. Combine frankfurters, soup, sour cream, and milk; mix well; pour over noodles. Bake in a hot oven (400°) about 25 minutes. Sprinkle bacon and peas over top; bake 5 minutes more.

Pichelsteiner Topf

Mixed meat and vegetables stew

6 servings

- *4 slices bacon, diced*
- *4 carrots, peeled and quartered*
- *2 large onions, sliced*
- *½ pound beef, cut into 1″ cubes*
- *½ pound lamb, cut into 1″ cubes*
- *½ pound pork, cut into 1″ cubes*
- *3 large potatoes, peeled and cubed*
- *4 cups beef bouillon*
- *½ teaspoon salt*
- *¼ teaspoon black pepper*
- *¼ teaspoon dried marjoram*
- *2 tablespoons chopped parsley*

Cook bacon in large Dutch oven until crisp; drain off fat. Place alternate layers of carrots, onions, meat and potatoes in Dutch oven. Add bouillon, salt, pepper and marjoram. Bring to a boil; cover; reduce heat and simmer about 1½ hours. Garnish with parsley before serving.

Sauerkraut-Auflauf

Sauerkraut and frankfurter casserole

6 servings

- *2 tablespoons salad oil*
- *1 cup sliced onion, about 2 medium*
- *1 (1 lb.) can sauerkraut*
- *¼ cup beef bouillon or water*
- *¼ pound sausage meat*
- *¼ cup dehydrated potato flakes*
- *⅓ cup Liebfraumilch wine*
- *½ teaspoon sugar*
- *3 slices bacon, cut into 1″ pieces*
- *2 small tart apples, cored, peeled and cut into ½″ rings*
- *2 cups mashed potatoes*
- *¼ pound (2–2½) frankfurters, sliced into ½″ pieces*
- *2 tablespoons margarine or butter*

Heat oil in large skillet. Sauté onions in hot fat over medium heat, until transparent. Add sauerkraut and bouillon. Cover; simmer about 25–30 minutes or until liquid has almost completely evaporated. Break up sausage meat into small pieces; stir into sauerkraut mixture; blend in potato flakes, then wine and sugar. Bring to a boil; simmer 1 minute; set aside. Fry bacon until browned. Remove bacon pieces; drain on paper towels. Add apple rings; sauté until browned and tender, about 2–3 minutes. Spread 1 cup mashed potatoes in bottom of greased 2-quart casserole. Cover with half the sauerkraut mixture; then the apples and bacon pieces. Spread remaining sauerkraut over these. Top with remaining mashed potatoes. Dot with margarine. Bake in a moderate oven (350°) 45 minutes or until potatoes are lightly browned.

Himmel und Erde

Heaven and earth

4–6 servings

- *1 teaspoon grated lemon rind*
- *2½ cups (28 oz. jar) applesauce*
- *2 cups mashed hot potatoes*
- *¼ pound bacon, diced*
- *2 large onions, sliced*
- *½ teaspoon salt*
- *⅛ teaspoon black pepper*
- *Blood sausage slices, or liver slices, cooked*

Stir lemon rind into applesauce. Mix with hot potatoes. Keep hot. Fry bacon in large skillet. Add sliced onions, cook over medium heat until transparent and golden brown. Stir into hot potato mixture. Add salt and pepper. Serve hot with hot blood sausage slices or liver.

Berliner Linsentopf

Lentils and bacon

8 servings

- *2¼ cups (1 lb.) lentils, washed and cleaned*
- *6 cups water*
- *1 pound thick sliced bacon, cut into 1″ pieces*
- *3 medium-sized potatoes (1 pound) peeled, cut into ½″ cubes*
- *½ cup vinegar*
- *¼ cup sugar*
- *Salt, if needed*
- *2 tablespoons margarine or butter*
- *2 medium onions, finely chopped*
- *2 tablespoons chopped parsley*

Combine lentils, water and bacon in large heavy saucepan. Bring to a boil; reduce heat. Cover; simmer 45 minutes. Add potatoes, continue to cook until lentils and potatoes are tender, about 15 minutes. Stir in vinegar and sugar. Taste, add salt, if needed. Place in serving dish; keep hot. Melt margarine in skillet; sauté onions and parsley over medium heat until onions are transparent, 2–3 minutes. Spoon over lentils. Serve hot.

Köthener Schusterpfanne

Shoemaker's pot

4 servings

- *2 pounds boneless pork loin roast*
- *1 teaspoon salt*
- *⅛ teaspoon pepper*
- *3 large potatoes, peeled and cut into 1″ cubes*
- *3 large green ripe pears, peeled and cut into eighths or 12 small ripe pears, peeled, cored, and halved*
- *¼ teaspoon dried marjoram*
- *¼ teaspoon dried dill weed*
- *1 tablespoon caraway seed*
- *1 tablespoon thick liquid beef broth and seasoning base*
- *2 cups boiling water*
- *2 tablespoons cornflour*
- *¼ cup cold water*

Sprinkle pork with salt and pepper; place in Dutch oven. Arrange potatoes and pears around meat. Sprinkle marjoram, dill and caraway seed over all. Dissolve seasoning base in boiling water; pour into Dutch oven; cover tightly. Bring to a boil; reduce heat; simmer about 1½ hours or until meat is tender when pierced with a fork. Remove meat, potatoes and pears to a warm platter. Stir cornflour into cold water. Add to liquid in Dutch oven. Cook over medium heat, stirring constantly, until sauce is thickened. Serve over meat.

Labskaus

Corned beef hash with egg

4 servings

- *2 (15½ oz.) cans corned beef hash*
- *½ cup chopped dill pickle*
- *½ cup chopped pickled herring*
- *2 tablespoons margarine or butter*
- *4 fried or poached eggs*

Combine hash, pickles, and herring; mix lightly. Melt margarine in large skillet. Spoon hash mixture into skillet; spread evenly in pan. Cook over low heat, stirring occasionally until hash is well browned. Top each serving of hash with a cooked egg.

'Labskaus' (corned beef hash) is an ancient sailor's dish which originated on the vessels coasting along the north coast of Germany and Scandinavia (recipe page 65, 4th column).

Cabbage and bacon casserole

Rothenburger Krautbraten

Cabbage and bacon casserole

4–6 servings

- 1 *medium head white cabbage, core removed*
- 1 *bay leaf*
- 9 *slices bacon*
- 1½ *pounds potatoes, diced*
- 1 *pound ground beef*
- ½ *cup coarse white bread crumbs*
- 1 *teaspoon salt*
- ⅛ *teaspoon pepper*
- ½ *teaspoon paprika*
- 1 *teaspoon caraway seed*
- ½ *cup top of milk*
- 2 *egg yolks*
- 2 *tablespoons flour*
- ½ *teaspoon salt*
- *Dash black pepper*

Cook whole cabbage in boiling salted water to which bay leaf has been added, about 5 minutes, or until outside cabbage leaves are tender. Drain well; carefully remove 5 or 6 outside cabbage leaves. Cut remaining cabbage into thin strips. Line a 5-quart casserole with bacon slices. Arrange cabbage leaves over bacon. Spread half the potatoes over cabbage leaves, Mix together beef, bread crumbs, salt, pepper, paprika and caraway seed. Alternate layers of meat mixture and finely cut cabbage. Cover with remaining potatoes. Beat together cream, egg yolks, flour, salt and pepper; pour over potatoes. Cover tightly. Bake in a moderate oven (350°) 45–60 minutes, or until potatoes are tender. Serve hot.

Vegetable dishes and dumplings

'Leipziger Allerlei' (a little of everything) is a dish prepared in the spring that uses all the many kinds of tender vegetables available in that season (recipe page 68, 2nd column).

Nature often cooperates with cookery by arranging it so that different things which go well together grow next to each other. A nice instance of this occurs on the left bank of the Rhine between Worms and Nierstein. Here, in this wide valley, the thickest, whitest and most tender asparagus imaginable grow right alongside the grapevines that yield the soft, blond luxurious wines from Rheinhessen. Liebfraumilch is the most famous of these wines. Asparagus and wine make up one of the gourmet's favorite combinations. The small hotels and inns in Oppenheim and Worms serve these asparagus accompanied by a sparkling white wine in wide glasses on brown stems. To eat these superb asparagus in the grand manner, you can go aboard a Rheindampfer, one of the large white boats which make day trips up and down the Rhine. Here, from the large windows of the ship's dining room, you can regard the slowly moving landscape of green hills and old castles and enjoy the tender asparagus while the sun sparkles in your glass.

Leipziger Allerlei

Vegetable medley

8 servings

2 cups beef bouillon
1 (10 oz.) package frozen cauliflower, separated
1 (10 oz.) package frozen peas
1 (10 oz.) package frozen asparagus, cut in half
1 (14 oz.) can baby carrots, drained
1 (3 oz.) can sliced mushrooms
4 tablespoons flour
2 teaspoons salt
¼ cup cold water
2 hard cooked eggs, peeled and quartered

Heat bouillon in large saucepan. Add vegetables; simmer 8–10 minutes. Add flour and salt to water; blend until smooth; stir into vegetables. Cook over low heat, stirring constantly, until thickened. Pour into serving dish. Garnish with eggs.

Rheinische Puffer

Rhenish potato pancakes

3 dozen 3″ pancakes

2 pounds large potatoes, peeled and cut into 2″ pieces
1 medium onion, cut into 6 wedges
2 eggs
1 teaspoon salt
Cooking oil

Break eggs into blender jar; start blending at high speed. Partially covering top, add one piece of potato at a time, 1–2 seconds apart, adding a piece of onion frequently. Add salt. Blend one minute. Heat a thin film of oil in griddle or skillet over moderately high heat. Add more oil as needed. For each pancake, spread a heaping tablespoon potato mixture into a 3″ circle; brown on both sides. Drain on paper towels. Keep warm until all are completed. Serve immediately.

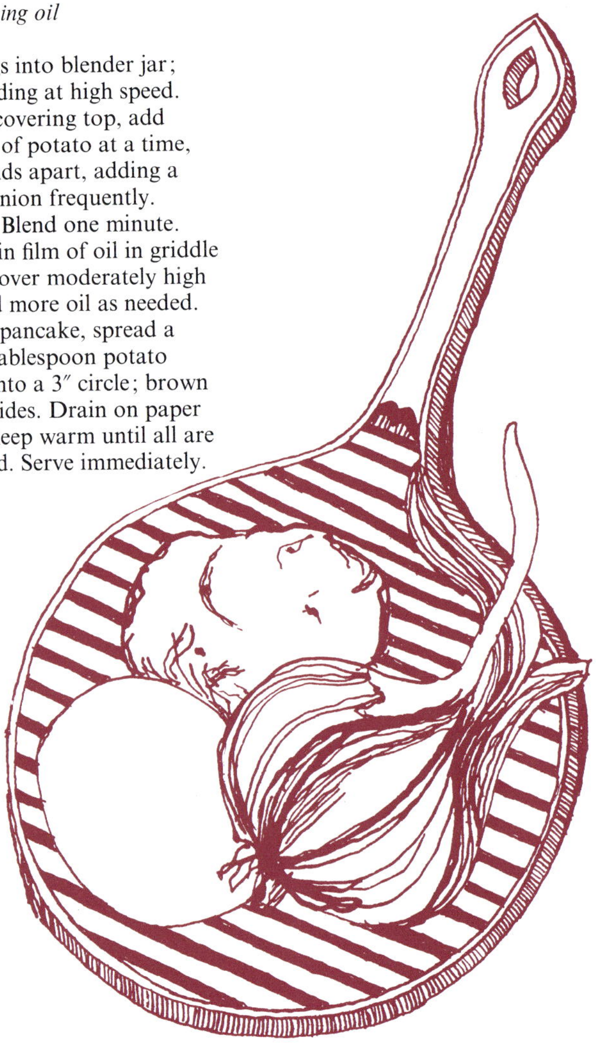

Sauerkraut

Braised sauerkraut

4 servings

- ¼ *cup margarine or butter*
- 1 *medium onion, chopped*
- 3 *cups sauerkraut, drained*
- 2 *cups beef bouillon*
- 2 *apples, sliced*
- 2 *slices bacon*
- 1 *potato, grated*

Melt margarine in large skillet. Sauté onion until golden brown. Stir in sauerkraut and apple slices. Pour in bouillon and place bacon slices on top. Cover; simmer for 30–40 minutes. Add grated potato and continue to simmer until mixture thickens, stirring constantly. Remove bacon and serve hot.

Schwäbische Spätzle

Tiny dumplings

4–6 servings

- 2 *eggs, slightly beaten*
- 1 *cup water*
- 1 *teaspoon salt*
- 3 *cups flour*

Combine eggs, water, salt, and flour. Beat until dough is thick and smooth. Add more flour if necessary. In a large saucepan, bring 2–3 quarts of salted water to a boil. Place ⅓ of the dough on a small, wet chopping board. With a sharp knife, cut thin strips (¾″ × 2½″) one at a time, slipping off board directly into boiling water. Repeat until all dough is used. Do not crowd in boiling water. Dumplings are done when they float. Remove from boiling water; rinse with hot water and keep warm. Serve with meat and gravy.

Lappenpickert

Potato cake

6–8 servings

- 4 *cups firmly packed, peeled, grated and drained potatoes (about 2 lbs.)*
- 2 *eggs, slightly beaten*
- 3 *tablespoons flour*
- 1 *teaspoon salt*
- ⅓ *cup sour cream*
- ¼ *cup salad oil*

Put grated potatoes into mixing bowl. Add eggs, flour, salt and sour cream. Beat with mixing spoon until well blended. Heat 2 tablespoons of the oil in each of 2 large skillets until very hot. Carefully spread half the potato mixture in each skillet, about ½″ thick. Cook over moderately high heat until browned on bottom. Carefully turn over. (If necessary, cut into quarters and turn each quarter separately.) Add more oil, if needed. Cook until browned. Serve immediately. If desired, wrap cooled potato sections in waxed paper. May be reheated in a little oil over moderate heat. Serve either as a meat accompaniment or with jelly or syrup.

Stangenspargel

Buttered asparagus

4 servings

- 2 *pounds fresh green or white asparagus*
- 1½ *teaspoons salt*
- 1 *teaspoon sugar*
- ¼ *cup melted margarine or butter*
- 1 *hard cooked egg, finely chopped, optional*

Arrange asparagus in 2 layers in 9″ or 10″ skillet. Sprinkle with salt and sugar. Pour on 1″ boiling water. Boil, uncovered, 5 minutes; cover and cook 7–10 minutes longer, or until just tender crisp when tested with a fork. Carefully lift out asparagus; arrange on serving dish. Pour melted margarine over asparagus. Garnish with chopped egg if desired.

Spinach filled pancakes

Westphalian white cabbage

Pfälzer Pfannkuchen-Auflauf

Spinach filled pancakes

4 servings

- *1 cup biscuit-type baking mix*
- *1 egg*
- *¾ cup milk*
- *1 (10 oz.) package frozen spinach, cooked and drained*
- *2 tablespoons margarine or butter*
- *⅛ teaspoon salt*
- *⅛ teaspoon black pepper*
- *Dash nutmeg*
- *½ cup evaporated milk*
- *1 cup (4 oz.) shredded Swiss cheese*

Combine baking mix, egg and milk; beat until smooth. Drop by ⅓ cup measures onto hot griddle. Cook over low heat until rim is full of broken bubbles; turn; brown on other side. Remove; keep warm. Combine spinach, margarine, salt, pepper and nutmeg; mix well. Spread spinach mixture on pancakes; roll. Place in greased 11¾″ × 7½″ × 1¾″ baking dish. Heat evaporated milk; add cheese. Cook, stirring constantly, until cheese is melted; pour over pancakes. Bake in a hot oven (400°) about 8–10 minutes or until lightly browned.

Westfälischer Weißkohl

Westphalian white cabbage

4–6 servings

- *4 tablespoons margarine or butter*
- *4 medium onions, chopped*
- *1 small head cabbage, chopped*
- *2 green apples, peeled and chopped*
- *1 tablespoon vinegar*
- *1 teaspoon sugar*
- *1 teaspoon salt*
- *¼ teaspoon black pepper*
- *2¾ cups hot water*
- *¼ cup instant mashed potato*

Melt margarine in skillet; add onion and cook until golden brown. In a large saucepan, make alternate layers of cabbage and apple. Add vinegar, sugar, salt and pepper. Pour 2 cups of the hot water over cabbage mixture. Cover tightly, bring to a boil, and simmer for 30 minutes. Add instant potatoes to remaining ¾ cup hot water. Stir potatoes and onion into hot cabbage. Serve warm.

Because we almost always eat cucumber raw, we sometimes forget that it makes an excellent dish when braised.

Hannoversches Gurkengemüse

Braised cucumbers

4 servings

¼ cup margarine or butter
1 tablespoon sugar
½ teaspoon salt
2 large cucumbers, peeled and cut into 2″ pieces
1 medium onion, chopped
2 tomatoes, quartered
¼ cup water
1 teaspoon lemon juice
¼ teaspoon dill weed
½ cup sour cream

Melt margarine in large saucepan. Add sugar and salt; cook until lightly browned. Add cucumbers and onion. Cook, stirring constantly, until onions are transparent. Add tomatoes, water, lemon juice, and dill weed. Cook 10–12 minutes. Stir in sour cream. Serve immediately.

Bayerische Kartoffelknödel

Bavarian potato dumplings

Makes 18

1 (14 oz.) loaf day-old French bread
1 cup milk
2 eggs, beaten
1 teaspoon salt
⅓ cup finely chopped onions
1 tablespoon parsley
3 quarts salted water

Cut bread into very thin slices; soak in milk. Add eggs and salt; let stand 30 minutes. Add onion and parsley. Blend to an even consistency. In a large, wide saucepan, bring salted water to a boil; reduce to a simmer. Shape dumplings with wet hands to about the size of a small egg. (If mixture is too soft, add some dry bread crumbs to it.) Drop dumplings into simmering water, being careful not to crowd dumplings. Cover and simmer for 10–15 minutes. Keep warm. Serve with meat and gravy.

Leberknödel

Liver dumplings

4–6 servings

½ pound baby beef liver, trimmed
2 cups packaged stuffing mix
1 cup warm water
¼ pound bacon, diced
1 large onion, chopped
2 eggs
1 teaspoon salt
Salted water or bouillon

Put liver through meat grinder. Soften stuffing mix in warm water. Fry bacon; add onion; cook over medium heat until onion is transparent. Mix together liver, softened stuffing, cooked bacon and onion, eggs and salt. (Add a little crushed dry stuffing mix if not quite firm enough to hold its shape.) Drop by ½ teaspoonfuls into gently boiling salted water or bouillon. Cook until tender, about 10 minutes. (Dumplings will rise to surface of water when done.) Serve with melted margarine or butter, if desired.

Bayerische Semmelknödel

Bavarian bread dumplings

6–8 servings

2 pounds potatoes, peeled and boiled
⅓ cup margarine or butter
⅛ teaspoon salt
1 egg yolk
¾ to 1 cup sifted flour
1 slice white bread, cut into 1″ cubes
1 tablespoon margarine or butter

Mash potatoes until very smooth with margarine and salt. Beat in egg and flour adding enough flour to make an easily handled dough. Fry cubes of bread in 1 tablespoon margarine, browning both sides. Form approximately 2″ balls of the potato dough. Press a cube of fried bread into center of each potato ball and smooth surface. Bring a large kettle of water to a boil. Drop potato balls carefully into boiling water. Bring water back to a boil, lower heat and simmer for 20 minutes. Dumplings should float and be slightly puffed up when done. Drain on paper towels. Serve immediately with sauerbraten or pot roast and gravy.

Buttered asparagus (recipe page 69, 4th column)

Bread dumplings with mushrooms. On any fine Sunday near the end of the summer or the beginning of fall, you can see German children roaming through the woods with baskets under their arms. They collect mushrooms, especially the beautiful, orange-yellow 'Pfifferlinge' which are always eaten with bread dumplings.

Semmelknödel mit Pilzen

Bread dumplings with mushrooms

4–6 servings

- 1 *recipe bread dumplings, page 72*
- ¼ *cup margarine or butter*
- 1 *pound fresh mushrooms, sliced*
- ½ *cup chopped parsley*
- 2 *tablespoons flour*
- 1 *cup top of milk*
- ½ *teaspoon salt*
- *Dash black pepper*

Prepare dumplings according to recipe on page 72. Meanwhile, melt margarine in large skillet. Sauté mushrooms in margarine until tender, about 10 minutes. Add parsley. Sprinkle flour over mushrooms. Gradually stir in top of milk. Cook over medium heat, stirring constantly, until thickened. Season with salt and pepper. Serve over dumplings.

Pastry

Apfelkuchen mit Guß

Apple custard cake

One 8″ square cake

- *½ cup margarine or butter*
- *¼ cup sugar*
- *1 teaspoon cinnamon*
- *1 cup sifted flour*
- *1 egg*
- *1 (3 oz.) package vanilla pudding mix*
- *1½ cups milk*
- *1 (22 oz.) can apple pie filling*
- *1 tablespoon lemon juice*
- *½ teaspoon grated lemon rind*

Beat margarine and sugar well; add cinnamon and blend in flour. Divide dough in half. Press one half into buttered 8″ square baking pan. Add egg to other half; mix well. Prepare vanilla pudding according to package directions, using 1½ cups milk. Pour half over dough in pan. Stir lemon juice and rind into apple pie filling. Spread over vanilla pudding. Cover apples with remaining vanilla pudding. Sprinkle reserved crumbly egg-flour mixture evenly over pudding. Bake in a moderate oven (350°) for 35 minutes, or until top is lightly browned. Cool. Cut in squares. Serve warm or cool.

Badische Apfelrolle

Baden apple roll

8 servings

- *1 (10 oz.) package frozen puff pastry tarts, thawed*
- *½ cup orange marmalade*
- *3 medium apples, peeled and sliced*
- *2 tablespoons chopped almonds*
- *2 tablespoons raisins*
- *2 tablespoons sugar*
- *1 teaspoon cinnamon*

Press dough together; roll out in a large rectangle about 12″ × 8″. Spread marmalade on surface of dough, leaving a 1″ margin on all sides. Place apples on top of marmalade on half of the dough. Sprinkle chopped almonds, raisins, sugar, and cinnamon on the apple slices. Fold other half of pastry over apples. Bake in a hot oven (400°) for 30–35 minutes or until pastry is lightly browned.

Schwäbischer Apfelkuchen

Swabian apple cake

9″ cake

- *2 cups flour*
- *1 cup sugar*
- *½ teaspoon salt*
- *1 cup margarine or butter*
- *1 egg, slightly beaten*
- *4 medium apples, sliced*
- *1 tablespoon lemon juice*
- *1 teaspoon lemon rind*
- *⅓ cup raisins*
- *½ cup almonds, chopped*

Mix flour, ¼ cup of the sugar, and salt. Cut in ¾ cup of the margarine until size of grains of cornmeal. Stir in egg until dough forms a ball. Gather together with fingers, if necessary; knead together to form a smooth dough. Chill. Role ⅔ of dough out on lightly floured board to make an 11″ round. Fit into a 9″ round cake pan. Combine apple slices, lemon juice and rind, raisins, and ½ of the almonds. Fill pastry-lined pan with mixture. Roll remaining pastry into 9″ round. Place on top of apples. Pinch edges together. Heat remaining margarine, sugar, and almonds together in a small saucepan slowly until margarine melts and sugar dissolves. Spoon over top crust of cake. Place in moderate oven (350°) and bake for 45–50 minutes or until crust is golden brown.

Germany has long been known for its many different kinds of pastry, but the most traditional are the 'Lebkuchen', golden-brown cakes, sweetened with honey and flavored with anise and other spices. They are sold at fairs and carnivals and at the Christmas markets.
These delicacies are baked in an endless array of shapes and forms, and many German museums have preserved cookie-boards of complex design that have been used to bake Lebkuchen for centuries. There are horses and carriages, hunters with their catch on their back, Saint Nicholas and the Christ Child, baskets of flowers, castles, Biblical scenes such as Adam and Eve in the garden of Eden, and the martyrdom of the Innocents at Bethlehem, and also lighter themes depicting Susan bathing, or a couple tenderly embracing each other.
Alas, this rich fantasy has given way to standard depictions of Saint Nicholas and of hearts decorated with red and white sugar rings or roses.
A Carnival would still be incomplete without Lebkuchen, and they also play an important role in weddings and village feasts. Sometimes small mirrors or red ribbons are baked into the cakes.
The most delicious Lebkuchen come from Nurnberg, which was an important junction for the spice merchants in the Middle Ages. The fortunate local bakers

Nürnberger Lebkuchen

could therefore lay their hands on cinnamon and nutmeg, cloves and ginger, anise and cardamon – everything needed to prepare the most delicious Lebkuchen.

Christmas spice biscuits

2 dozen 2″ cookies

- *2 eggs*
- *1 cup sugar*
- *1 cup sifted flour*
- *¼ teaspoon cinnamon*
- *⅛ teaspoon ground cloves*
- *⅛ teaspoon powdered cardamom*
- *¾ cup blanched almonds, chopped fine in blender*
- *¼ cup candied lemon peel*
- *½ teaspoon grated lemon peel*

Beat eggs, gradually add sugar and beat until thickened. Blend in flour, spices, almonds and lemon peels. Drop by teaspoonful on well greased cookie sheets, or spread in a well greased 8″ square baking pan. Bake in a slow oven (325°) 15–20 minutes or until edges are beginning to brown for drop cookies; 20–25 minutes or until edges begin to pull away from sides of pan for bar cookies. Remove from cookie sheet; cool on rack. Or, cut into bars about 3″ × 1″ (make 3 cuts in one direction, 8 in the other). Cool on rack. Store cookies or bars in cookie jar to mellow for a few days. Cookies may be sprinkled with powdered sugar or iced with a chocolate glaze.

A good strudel is the pride of any Bavarian housewife. She probably stood around in the kitchen and learned the art from her mother when she was a small child.

Bayerischer Apfelstrudel

Bavarian apple strudel

18 servings

- *1 tablespoon oil*
- *1 egg*
- *1/3 cup warm water*
- *1/4 teaspoon salt*
- *1 1/2 cups sifted flour*
- *1/3 cup melted margarine or butter*
- *6 tablespoons fine dry bread crumbs*
- *8 cups thinly sliced, peeled and cored tart apples*
- *2 tablespoons dark rum*
- *3 tablespoons sugar*
- *1/2 teaspoon cinnamon*
- *1/4 cup finely chopped almonds*
- *1/4 cup seedless raisins*
- *Icing sugar or whipped cream, optional*

Beat together oil, egg, water and salt; add flour while beating, until a firm dough which pulls away from bowl is formed. Knead several times until smooth and elastic. Cover; let stand 30 minutes. Cut with sharp knife into two equal parts. Roll out each piece on floured cloth to a 12″ × 18″ rectangle. Brush with melted margarine. Sprinkle evenly with bread crumbs. Spread 4 cups of the apples on each portion, lengthwise down the center of the dough. Sprinkle each with 1 tablespoon rum, 1 1/2 tablespoons sugar, 1/4 teaspoon cinnamon, 2 tablespoons almonds and 2 tablespoons raisins. Fold dough over apples on one side, then the other. Slide rolls onto greased baking sheet. Brush with melted margarine. Bake in a hot oven (400°) 45 minutes. Cut each roll into 2″ slices. Serve warm or cold sprinkled with icing sugar or with whipped cream, if desired.

Zwetschgendatschi

Fresh plum cake

One 9″ × 13″ cake

- *2 pounds fresh blue plums*
- *1 package dry yeast*
- *1 cup milk, lukewarm*
- *3½ cups flour*
- *1 teaspoon salt*
- *1 cup sugar*
- *¼ cup margarine or butter*
- *1 egg, slightly beaten*
- *2 tablespoons margarine or butter*

Wash and gently cut plums in half, removing the pits. Sprinkle yeast into ¼ cup of the milk. Let stand until dissolved.
Mix flour, salt, and ⅓ cup of the sugar in a large bowl. Stir dissolved yeast, margarine, egg, and remaining milk into flour. Knead into a soft dough.
Let rise for 30–40 minutes in a warm place. Punch down and roll on a lightly floured board into an oblong about 9″ × 13″. Fit into a greased pan of that size. Pinch edges to make a slight edge around all sides.
Let rise for 20 minutes. Place plums on top with cut side up. Sprinkle with remaining sugar; dot with margarine. Bake in a moderate oven (350°) for 35–40 minutes. Slice and serve warm.

Black forest cherry cake (recipe page 78, 1st column)

Fresh plum cake

Schwarzwälder Kirschtorte

Black forest cherry cake

One 8″ layer cake

- ½ *cup margarine or butter*
- ½ *cup sugar*
- 3 *eggs*
- ½ *cup almonds, finely chopped in blender*
- 1 *(6-oz.) package cooking chocolate, chopped fine in blender*
- 1 *teaspoon vanilla*
- ¾ *cup sifted cake flour*
- 1 *teaspoon baking powder*
- ½ *teaspoon salt*
- 1 *cup heavy cream*
- 2 *tablespoons honey*
- ½ *cup Kirschwasser or ½ cup cherry brandy*
- 2 *(1 lb.) cans sour pitted cherries, well-drained Maraschino cherries*

Cream together margarine and sugar until light and fluffy; add eggs one at a time, beating well after each addition. Beat in almonds, ¾ cup of the chopped chocolate, and vanilla. Sift together flour, baking powder and salt. Stir into butter mixture. Divide evenly between three greased, waxed-paper-lined and re-greased 8″ layer cake pans. Bake in a moderately hot oven (375°) about 20 minutes, or until edges start to pull away from sides of pan. Cool on cake rack about 10 minutes. Turn out; remove waxed paper. Cool cake layers on cake rack. Whip cream with honey until stiff. Place one cake layer on serving plate; sprinkle with one-third of the liquer; spread with one-third of the whipped cream; cover evenly with one-half of the sour cherries. Place second layer on top, pressing down slightly. Repeat as for first layer. Top with third layer, press down slightly, sprinkle with liquer, cover with whipped cream. Decorate top and sides with reserved ¼ cup chopped chocolate and Maraschino cherries. Chill well before serving.

Streuselkuchen

Streusel coffee cake

One 13″ × 9″ cake

- 1 *package hot roll mix*
- ¼ *cup margarine or butter, melted*
- 1 *cup flour*
- 1 *cup sugar*
- 2 *teaspoons cinnamon*
- 1 *teaspoon grated lemon rind*
- ½ *cup margarine or butter*

Prepare hot roll mix according to package directions. After first rising, knead and roll into large rectangle 13″ × 9″. Fit into a buttered pan of equal size. Brush top with melted margarine. Put in warm place until dough rises to double original size. Combine flour, sugar, cinnamon, and lemon rind. Cut in margarine with pastry blender or two knives. Spread over surface of buttered dough. Bake in moderate oven (350°) for 40–45 minutes or until browned.

Feiner Sahnekuchen

Delicate sour cream cake

One 9″ × 13″ × 2″ cake

- 1 *(13¾ oz.) package hot roll mix*
- 2 *tablespoons soft margarine or butter*
- ½ *cup sugar*
- 1 *pint sour cream*
- 4 *tablespoons sugar*
- 1 *teaspoon vanilla*

Prepare hot roll mix according to package directions, adding margarine and ½ cup sugar when adding the egg called for in package directions. Cover; allow to rise in a warm place until doubled in size, about 30–45 minutes. Knead lightly on a floured surface several times until dough is no longer sticky. Roll or press out with fingers to fit a buttered 9″ × 13″ × 2″ pan. Place in pan. Mix together sour cream, sugar and vanilla. Spread over surface of dough. Let rise in warm place until doubled, about 30–45 minutes. Bake in a moderate oven (350°) about 35–45 minutes or until edges are browned. Allow to cool at least 30 minutes before cutting into squares.

Bienenstich

"Bee sting" cake

One 15″ × 10″ × 1″ cake

- *1 package hot roll mix*
- *1 cup margarine or butter*
- *1 cup sugar*
- *1 (6 oz.) package slivered almonds*

Prepare hot roll mix according to package directions. After first rising, knead and roll into a large rectangle about 15″ × 10″. Place in a buttered pan of equal size. Put dough in a warm place and allow the dough to double in volume, about 20–30 minutes. Melt margarine. Pour ¼ cup over the surface of the dough. Add sugar to the rest of the margarine and beat until the sugar is dissolved. Mix in almonds. Spread mixture on top of buttered dough. Bake in a moderate oven (350°) for 35–40 minutes or until the top is lightly browned. Cool and cut in squares.

Prinzregententorte

Chocolate layer cake

One 8″ cake

- *1 (17-oz.) package pound cake mix*
- *½ cup softened margarine or butter*
- *1 (6-oz.) package cooking chocolate, melted*
- *2 eggs, separated*
- *1 cup sifted icing sugar*
- *3 squares unsweetened chocolate, melted*

Prepare cake mix according to package directions. Bake as follows: Grease and line with waxed paper, grease again, two 8″ round cake pans. Pour ¾ cup (1/5 of the batter) into each pan, spreading evenly. Bake in moderate oven (350°) until golden brown and edges pull away from sides of pan, about 30 minutes. Remove from pan and carefully peel off paper. Cool on rack. Bake three more layers in this way.

Filling: Beat margarine into melted cooking chocolate. Add egg yolks; beat until mixture is glossy and of spreading consistency. Spread filling between layers; press each layer down firmly. Cool until well set before frosting cake.

Frosting: Beat egg whites until foamy; beat in icing sugar gradually, until well blended. Stir in melted unsweetened chocolate. Spread over top and sides of cake. Cool.

You used to be able to buy Berlin doughnuts along the streets from a man pushing a small cart bearing large lined glass jars. The glass was always misted in winter because of the steam from the hot cakes inside.

Berliner Pfannkuchen

Berlin style jelly doughnuts

Makes 18–20

3½ cups flour
¼ cup sugar
1 teaspoon salt
1 package yeast
1 cup milk, lukewarm
2 tablespoons salad oil
1 egg, slightly beaten
2 teaspoons rum
1 egg white, slightly beaten
Marmalade
Oil or fat for deep frying
1 cup icing sugar

Sift flour, sugar and salt. Soften yeast in ¼ cup of the warm milk. Stir in ¾ of flour mixture. Add oil, egg, and rum. Add remaining flour mixture. Work into soft dough. Cover and let rise in a warm place for 45 minutes to 1 hour. Punch down and roll out on floured board into ½″ thickness. Cut into 3″ rounds. Place 1 teaspoon of marmalade in center of each round. Brush edges with egg white. Pinch edges together to seal completely. Place balls on floured surface, smooth side up; let rise 20 minutes. Heat oil to 360°; fry doughnuts a few at a time until browned on one side then turn over (about 3–4 minutes on each side). Remove from oil with slotted spoon and drain on paper towels. Sprinkle with icing sugar.

Christmas is not complete without marzipan hanging on the Christmas tree. You can buy this delicious treat in Christmas markets all over Germany.

Schlesische Käsetaschen

Silesian cheese cases

6 servings

- 1 *(10 oz.) package frozen puff pastry, thawed*
- 1 *(3 oz.) package cream cheese, softened*
- ½ *cup creamed cottage cheese*
- 2 *tablespoons sugar*
- ½ *cup raisins*
- 1 *egg yolk*

Roll out pastry shells to approximately 8″ diameter. Beat together cream cheese, cottage cheese, sugar, raisins and egg yolk. Divide cheese filling in 6 equal portions, placing one in center of each round. Bring 6 equidistant points on outer edge to center, one at a time, moistening with water and pressing together lightly to seal. Place cases on ungreased cookie sheet. Preheat oven to 450°. Place cookie sheet into oven and immediately lower temperature to 375°. Bake until golden brown, about 30 minutes. Remove from cookie sheet. If desired, drizzle a glaze of 1 cup icing sugar mixed with 1–2 tablespoons water over cases while still warm. Cool.

Königsberger Marzipan

Almond paste cookies

Makes 30 2″ cookies

Cookies:

- 3 *cups finely ground blanched almonds*
- 1 *pound icing sugar*
- 1 *teaspoon almond extract*
- 4 *tablespoons orange juice*
- 1 *egg white*

Icing:

- 1 *cup icing sugar*
- 1½ *tablespoons orange juice*
- *Candied cherries, halved*
- *Angelica, cut in strips*

Mix together almonds, icing sugar, almond extract, and orange juice. Knead until thoroughly blended. Shape into a large, flat rectangle. Wrap in aluminum foil and chill for several hours. Divide dough in half. Roll out to a thickness of ⅛″ on a board heavily dusted with icing sugar. Cut out hearts, using 2″ heart cutter. Cut centers out of half of the hearts, using a smaller heart cookie cutter. Place whole hearts on a well buttered baking sheet. Top with heart-shaped rims. Press together with prongs of a fork. Bake in very hot oven (450°) until lightly browned. Brush with egg white. Cool thoroughly. For icing, mix icing sugar and orange juice until smooth. Frost centers with icing. Decorate with cherry halves and angelica strips.

Thüringer Kirschkuchen

Cherry cake

One 10″ cake

- *1 (16 oz.) can sour cherries, pitted*
- *4 eggs, separated*
- *1 cup sugar*
- *1 teaspoon grated lemon rind*
- *1½ cups flour*
- *1½ teaspoons baking powder*
- *½ teaspoon salt*
- *1 teaspoon cinnamon*
- *1 (6 oz.) package almonds finely chopped*
- *1 tablespoon margarine or butter*
- *¼ cup fine dry bread crumbs*

Drain cherries, reserving ½ cup juice. Beat egg yolks, gradually adding sugar, lemon rind, and cherry juice. Sift flour, baking powder, salt, and cinnamon together. Stir flour into egg yolk mixture, blending well. Beat egg whites until stiff, but not dry. Gently fold egg whites into batter. Fold in chopped almonds. Pour into 10″ bundt pan, well buttered, and then sprinkled with dry bread crumbs. Sprinkle cherries evenly over top. Bake in moderate oven (350°) for 45–50 minutes, or until cake is lightly browned and springs back when gently touched with finger.

Quark-Keilchen

Fried cheese cakes

6 servings

- *2 cups (1 lb.) creamed cottage cheese*
- *½ cup dehydrated potato flakes*
- *2 eggs*
- *⅛ teaspoon salt*
- *⅓ cup sugar*
- *½ teaspoon grated lemon rind*
- *⅓ cup raisins*
- *1 cup sifted flour*
- *¼ cup margarine or butter icing sugar, syrup or preserves*

Mix together cottage cheese, potato flakes, eggs, salt, sugar, lemon rind, raisins and flour to form a smooth dough, adding a little more flour if dough is too sticky. Pat the dough out on a floured surface to form a rectangle 9″ × 3″. Cut into 1½″ squares. Melt margarine in frying pan over medium heat. Fry squares on both sides until browned, about 1–2 minutes on each side. Serve hot with icing sugar, syrup or preserves.

Dresdener Christstollen

Dresden Christmas fruit bread

2 loaves

- *2 envelopes dry yeast*
- *1 cup lukewarm milk*
- *5 to 5½ cups sifted flour*
- *2 eggs*
- *½ teaspoon salt*
- *½ teaspoon almond extract*
- *1 cup margarine or butter, softened*
- *½ cup sugar*
- *¼ cup chopped candied lemon or orange peel*
- *⅔ cup seedless raisins*
- *⅔ cup dried currants*
- *½ cup slivered, blanched almonds*
- *½ cup melted margarine or butter*
- *⅔ cup icing sugar*

In mixing bowl, stir yeast into milk. Stir to dissolve. Add 4 cups of the flour, eggs, salt and almond extract; beat until smooth dough is formed. Sprinkle with about 1 tablespoon of the flour. Let stand in a warm place until doubled in bulk, about 30–45 minutes. Punch dough down, place on a lightly floured surface, knead in softened margarine, sugar, and remaining flour until smooth and well-blended. Knead in lemon or orange peel, raisins, currants and almonds. Divide into two equal portions. Roll out each to an oval shape about ¾″ thick and 9″ × 6″ at the widest points. Fold one long side about ¾ of the way over the other. Gently press the edges together to make a loaf about 3–3½″ wide by 9″ long. Place on a greased baking sheet, cover and let rise in a warm place until doubled in bulk, about 30–45 minutes. Brush tops with half of the melted margarine. Bake in a moderately hot oven (400°) about 25–35 minutes or until golden brown. Brush with remaining margarine. Sprinkle with icing sugar.
Return to oven for 1 minute. Remove. Cool on rack.

Hutzelbrot

Spicy fruit loaf

One 9″ × 5″ × 3″ loaf

- *1 (12 oz.) package pitted, mixed, dried fruit, diced*
- *¼ cup raisins*
- *2 cups boiling water*
- *3 cups biscuit-type baking mix*
- *⅔ cup sugar*
- *⅓ cup flour*
- *1 teaspoon cinnamon*
- *⅛ teaspoon ground cloves*
- *1 egg*
- *⅔ cup milk*
- *⅓ cup Kümmel, Kirschwasser or fruit juice*
- *½ cup chopped nuts*
- *1 tablespoon castor sugar or 1 cup icing sugar*

In a bowl, pour boiling water over prepared fruit and raisins. Let stand while batter is being mixed. Stir together well, baking mix, sugar, flour, cinnamon and cloves. Add egg, milk and liquer or fruit juice. Beat vigorously about ½ minute or until well-blended. Drain fruit; reserve liquid. Stir fruit and nuts into batter. Pour batter into greased 9″ × 5″ × 3″ loaf pan. Bake in a moderate oven (350°) about 1 hour or until toothpick inserted near center comes out clean. Cool 10 minutes in pan. Remove from pan. Brush with reserved soaking liquid; sprinkle 1 tablespoon castor sugar over surface while hot. Cool. (Or, stir together 1 cup confectioners' sugar and 1–2 tablespoons liquid drained from fruit and 1 teaspoon liquer, if desired. Blend well. Glaze top of cake, letting mixture dribble down sides. Cool.)

'Beggar's' apple pudding

Frankfurter Bettelmann

"Beggar's" apple pudding

6 servings

- *10 slices day-old pumpernickel or rye bread, cubed*
- *1–1½ cups apple cider*
- *1 teaspoon cinnamon*
- *⅓ cup sugar*
- *2 pounds apples, peeled, cored, and sliced*
- *¼ cup raisins*
- *2 tablespoons margarine or butter*

Mix bread cubes with enough cider to moisten and soften. Combine cinnamon and sugar. Alternate layers of bread, apple slices, cinnamon, sugar, and raisins in a 2-qt. buttered casserole. End with a top layer of bread cubes. Dot top with margarine. Bake in moderate oven (350°) for 45 minutes. Serve with cream or vanilla ice cream.

You can make this delicious dessert with cranberries, but in Germany one always uses 'Preisselbeeren', small red berries that grow on low bushes in the woods. Their bitter-sour flavor goes very well with cranberries.

Pommersche Götterspeise

Cranberry pudding

4 servings

- ½ *cup cream*
- ¾ *tablespoon sugar*
- ¼ *teaspoon vanilla*
- 2 *slices pumpernickel or rye bread, crumbed*
- ⅔ *cup whole cranberry sauce*
- 1 *tablespoon pistachio nuts*

Whip the cream, gently adding sugar and vanilla. Make alternate layers of bread crumbs, cranberry sauce, and whipped cream in four dessert dishes. Chill thoroughly, at least two hours. Garnish with chopped nuts.

Bielefelder Schwarzbrotpudding

Rye bread and fruit pudding

8–10 servings

- *3 eggs, separated*
- *2/3 cup sugar*
- *1 teaspoon vanilla*
- *1/2 teaspoon cinnamon*
- *4 cups (6 slices) seedless rye bread, cubed*
- *1 pint fresh blueberries or cranberries*
- *1 (6 oz.) package cooking chocolate*
- *Top of milk if desired*

Beat egg whites until foamy. Gradually beat in 1/3 cup of the sugar and the vanilla, until stiff, but not dry. Beat egg yolks until thick; gradually beat in 1/3 cup of the sugar and cinnamon until mixture is very thick and forms a ribbon when beater is picked up.
Fold egg yolk mixture into egg whites. Fold egg mixture into cubed rye bread. Sprinkle half the berries in bottom of buttered 2-quart casserole. Spread one-third of bread mixture over berries. Sprinkle half of chocolate pieces over surface. Cover with another third of bread mixture. Sprinkle remaining berries over surface, cover with last third of bread mixture. Sprinkle remaining chocolate pieces on top.
Cover with lid or foil. Bake in moderately slow oven (325°) for about 1 hour, or until knife inserted one inch from edge comes out clean. Cool.
Unmold onto serving plate. Serve top of milk separately.

Versoffene Jungfern

"Drowned Maidens"

Makes about 4 dozen

- 3 *tablespoons margarine or butter*
- ⅓ *cup sugar*
- 6 *eggs, separated*
- ⅔ *cup sifted flour*
- ½ *teaspoon salt*
- *Oil for deep frying*
- *Icing sugar*

Cream margarine; gradually beat in sugar until well blended. Beat in egg yolks until smooth and thickened. Blend in flour and salt gently to form a smooth batter. Beat egg whites until stiff but not dry; fold into batter. Drop batter by teaspoonfuls into hot fat (400°). Fry until golden brown, about 1–2 minutes on each side, turning once. Drain on paper towels; sprinkle with icing sugar. Serve immediately.

Arme Ritter

"Poor Knight's" dessert

6 servings

- 1 *cup milk*
- 2 *eggs, beaten*
- 4 *tablespoons sugar*
- 1 *teaspoon vanilla*
- ½ *teaspoon grated lemon rind*
- 6 *slices day-old white bread*
- ⅓ *cup dry bread crumbs*
- 2 *tablespoons margarine or butter*
- ⅓ *cup sugar*
- ½ *teaspoon cinnamon*

Mix together milk, eggs, sugar, vanilla, and lemon rind. Dip bread slices first in egg mixture, then in dry bread crumbs. Melt margarine in large skillet and brown bread slices on both sides. Sprinkle with mixture of sugar and cinnamon. Serve warm.

Rote Grütze

Currant and raspberry pudding

4 servings

- 1 *(10-oz.) package quick-thaw frozen raspberries, thawed*
- 1 *(4-oz.) package currant and raspberry flavor pudding mix*
- *Light cream or top of milk*

Drain juice from frozen raspberries, measure and add water to make 2 cups. DO NOT USE MILK. Stir into pudding mix in saucepan. Bring to a boil. Boil one minute only, stirring constantly. Very gently, stir in drained raspberries. Pour into individual serving dishes. Chill 3 to 4 hours. Serve with cream or top of milk.

Brandied plum mold

Munich beer cream

White grape custard. The hillsides along the Saar river, a tributary of the Mosel, are planted with tender green grapevines. People along the Saar combine wine and grapes in a delicious, soft, creamy dessert.

Cognac Pflaumenpudding

Brandied plum mold

4–6 servings

- *1 (30 oz.) can purple plums*
- *2 envelopes unflavored gelatine*
- *½ cup cold water*
- *¼ cup sugar*
- *1 teaspoon grated lemon rind*
- *¼ cup lemon juice*
- *⅓ cup plum or cherry brandy*
- *¼ teaspoon cinnamon*
- *1 teaspoon vanilla*
- *½ cup chopped almonds*
- *½ cup heavy cream, whipped*

Drain plums; reserve and measure liquid. Pit and purée the plums in blender or through a food mill. Soften gelatine in cold water. Heat 1¾ cups plum liquid and sugar to the boiling point, stirring frequently; remove from heat. Stir in softened gelatine until dissolved. Stir in 1⅔ cups plum purée, lemon rind and juice, brandy, cinnamon and vanilla. Pour into 1½ quart mold which has been rinsed with cold water. Chill until firmly set, about 2–3 hours. Unmold on serving platter. Garnish with almonds and whipped cream.

Saarländer Becher

White grape custard

6–8 servings

- *½ cup seedless white grapes, halved*
- *½ cup sugar*
- *1 tablespoon cornflour*
- *1 teaspoon grated lemon rind*
- *1 tablespoon lemon juice*
- *2 cups sauterne wine*
- *4 eggs, lightly beaten*
- *Biscuits*

Divide grapes among individual serving dishes or place in serving bowl. Mix sugar and cornflour in top section of double boiler. Stir in lemon rind, lemon juice and wine. Cook over direct medium heat, stirring constantly, until mixture comes to a boil. Pour about half of the cooked mixture over the beaten eggs, stirring rapidly to blend. Return egg mixture to top of double boiler, blending with remaining wine mixture. Cook over hot but *not* boiling water, stirring constantly, until mixture thickens and coats a spoon, about 1 minute. Strain immediately and pour over grapes. Serve warm or chilled with a biscuit.

Münchner Biercreme

Munich beer cream

6 servings

- *1 cup mild dark beer*
- *¾ cup water*
- *½ cup sugar*
- *2 tablespoons lemon juice*
- *1 tablespoon unflavored gelatine*
- *4 eggs, separated*

In top of a double boiler, mix together beer, ½ cup of the water, sugar, and lemon juice. Sprinkle gelatine over remaining ¼ cup of water; mix to dissolve; add to beer mixture. Beat egg yolks slightly and stir into beer mixture. Place over simmering water. Cook, stirring constantly, until mixture coats a metal spoon, about 8–10 minutes. Cool. Beat egg whites until they stand in soft peaks. Fold egg whites into beer mixture. Pour into individual serving dishes and chill. Serve cold.

Mohrle im Hemd

Dark maidens in skirts

4–6 servings

1 cup margarine or butter
⅔ cup sugar
3 egg yolks
1 (6 oz.) package chocolate chips
1 cup milk
25–30 ladyfingers
2 tablespoons rum
½ cup cream, whipped

Cream margarine and sugar. Beat in egg yolks, continuing to beat until thoroughly blended. Melt chocolate bits in top of double boiler over hot (not boiling) water. Add milk, stirring to combine thoroughly. Cool. Gradually add chocolate milk to margarine mixture; stir until thoroughly blended. Sprinkle ladyfingers with rum. In a deep 2-qt. casserole, arrange alternate layers of ladyfingers and chocolate mixture. Chill thoroughly. Decorate with whipped cream. Serve cold.

The average German is evidently a thirsty man. Not only does he drink 140 liters of beer and 18 liters of wine per year, but Germany is also famous for its cold and warm fruit punch. During the summer, signs hanging in the gardens of the cafes along the Rhine, Moselle and Neckar rivers announce: 'cherry punch today'. On the white Rhine boats, the waiter prowls the deck with large glass mugs set in bowls with crushed ice and filled with sparkling, full-flavored 'Kalte Ente', a delicious drink made of white wine and fruit. Hot drinks such as 'Krambambuli' and 'Feuerzwangenbowl' were always the reward of hunters after they reached the comfort of their firesides on winter nights in their remote castles in the woods of East Prussia or Schleswig-Holstein.
These drinks were considered too strong for the ladies, however.
These same hot and potent drinks were traditional for warming up the student parties in Heidelberg when it was still the exclusive university for the sons of aristocrats. But that time is long gone. Krambambuli, Jägerspunch and Feuerzwangenbowl are still prepared and drunk, but the company is less exclusive and the ladies enjoy them now as well.

Krambambuli

Krambambuli

18 servings

- *½ gallon dry red wine*
- *¼ cup orange juice*
- *2 tablespoons lemon juice*
- *1 spiral orange peel*
- *1 stick cinnamon*
- *4 cloves*
- *8 tablespoons sugar*
- *⅓ cup rum*

Combine wine, juice, peel, cinnamon, cloves and 4 tablespoons sugar in saucepan. Simmer 8–10 minutes; strain into punch bowl. Heat rum slightly. Place remaining sugar in large metal spoon or ladle. Light rum with a match; pour over sugar. Pour burning sugar over punch.

Pfirsich-bowle

Peach cup

16 servings

- *4 ripe peaches, peeled, pitted and quartered*
- *¼ to ½ cup super fine sugar*
- *½ cup brandy*
- *2 bottles Rhine wine*
- *1 quart chilled club soda*

Place fruit in large pitcher; sprinkle with sugar. Add brandy; stir well. Stir in wine. Cover; chill 2–3 hours. Add club soda just before serving.

Kalte Ente

Cold duck

18 servings

- *½ cup super fine sugar*
- *1 large lemon, thinly sliced and seeded*
- *½ cup orange liqueur*
- *½ gallon Rhine wine, chilled*
- *Ice*
- *1 (12 oz.) bottle club soda, chilled*

Sprinkle sugar over lemon slices. Press lemon slices with back of spoon to release flavor. Stir in orange liqueur. Chill. Stir in wine; pour over ice in punch bowl. Add club soda; stir lightly to blend.

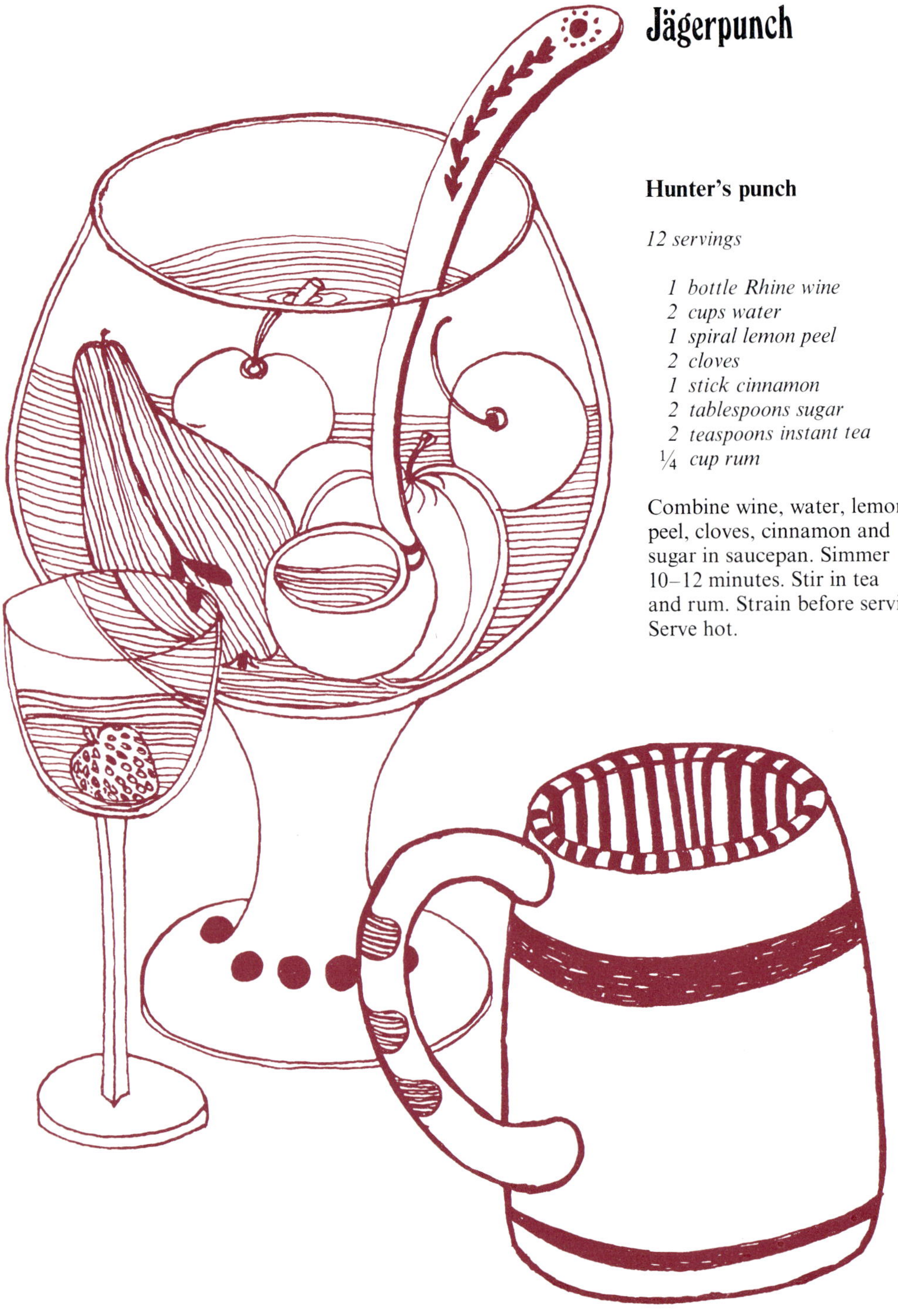

Jägerpunch

Hunter's punch

12 servings

- *1 bottle Rhine wine*
- *2 cups water*
- *1 spiral lemon peel*
- *2 cloves*
- *1 stick cinnamon*
- *2 tablespoons sugar*
- *2 teaspoons instant tea*
- *¼ cup rum*

Combine wine, water, lemon peel, cloves, cinnamon and sugar in saucepan. Simmer 10–12 minutes. Stir in tea and rum. Strain before serving. Serve hot.

Heißer Seehund

Hot seal

8 servings

- *1 bottle Rhine wine*
- *1¾ cup seedless golden raisins*
- *1 stick cinnamon*
- *1 spiral lemon peel*
- *¼ cup sugar*
- *¼ cup brandy*

Combine wine, raisins, cinnamon, lemon peel, and sugar in saucepan. Simmer 8–10 minutes. Remove lemon peel. Add brandy. Ladle into individual punch cups.

Conversion tables

Liquid measures

American standard cup | | **metric equivalent** (approximately)

American standard cup		metric equivalent (approximately)
1 cup = ½ pint	= 8 fl. oz. (fluid ounce)	= 2,37 dl (deciliter)
1 tbs. (tablespoon)	= ½ fl. oz.	= 1,5 cl (centiliter)
1 tsp. (teaspoon)	= ⅙ fl. oz.	= 0,5 cl
1 pint	= 16 fl. oz.	= 4,73 dl
1 quart = 2 pints	= 32 fl. oz.	= 9,46 dl

British standard cup		metric equivalent (approximately)
1 cup = ½ pint	= 10 fl. oz.	= 2,84 dl
1 tbs	= 0.55 fl. oz.	= 1,7 cl
1 tsp.	= ⅕ fl. oz.	= 0,6 cl
1 pint	= 20 fl. oz.	= 5,7 dl
1 quart = 2 pints	= 40 fl. oz.	= 1,1 l (liter)

1 cup = 16 tablespoons
1 tablespoon = 3 teaspoons

1 liter = 10 deciliter = 100 centiliter

Solid measures

American/British		metric equivalent (approximately)
1 lb. (pound)	= 16 oz. (ounces)	= 453 g (gram)
	1 oz.	= 28 g
2.2 lbs.		= 1000 g = 1 kg (kilogram)
	3½ oz.	= 100 g

Oven temperatures

Centigrade	Fahrenheit	
up to 105° C	up to 225° F	cool
105–135° C	225–275° F	very slow
135–160° C	275–325° F	slow
175–190° C	350–375° F	moderate
215–230° C	400–450° F	hot
230–260° C	450–500° F	very hot
260° C	500° F	extremely hot

Kitchen terms

Aspic
A stiff gelatine obtained by combining fish or meat bouillon with gelatine powder.

Au gratin
Obtained by covering a dish with a white sauce (usually prepared with grated cheese) and then heating the dish in the oven so that a golden crust forms.

Baste
To moisten meat or other foods while cooking to add flavor and to prevent drying of the surface. The liquid is usually melted fat, meat drippings, fruit juice or sauce.

Blanch (precook)
To preheat in boiling water or steam. (1) Used to inactivate enzymes and shrink food for canning, freezing, and drying. Vegetables are blanched in boiling water or steam, and fruits in boiling fruit juice, syrup, water, or steam. (2) Used to aid in removal of skins from nuts, fruits, and some vegetables.

Blend
To mix thoroughly two or more ingredients.

Bouillon
Brown stock, conveniently made by dissolving a bouillon cube in water.

Broth
Water in which meat, fish or vegetables have been boiled or cooked.

'En papillote'
Meat, fish or vegetables wrapped in grease-proof paper or aluminum foil (usually first sprinkled with oil or butter, herbs and seasonings) and then baked in the oven or grilled over charcoal. Most of the taste and aroma are preserved in this way.

Fold
To combine by using two motions, cutting vertically through the mixture and turning over and over by sliding the implement across the bottom of the mixing bowl with each turn.

Fry
To cook in fat; applied especially (1) to cooking in a small amount of fat, also called sauté or pan-fry; (2) to cooking in a deep layer of fat, also called deep-fat frying.

Marinate
To let food stand in a marinade usually an oil–acid mixture like French dressing.

Parboil
To boil until partially cooked. The cooking is usually completed by another method.

Poach
To cook in a hot liquid using precautions to retain shape. The temperature used varies with the food.

Reduce
To concentrate the taste and aroma of a particular liquid or food, e.g. wine, bouillon, soup, sauce etc. by boiling in a pan with the lid off so that the excess water can evaporate.

Roast
To cook, uncovered, by dry heat. Usually done in an oven, but occasionally in ashes, under coals or on heated stones or metals. The term is usually applied to meats but may refer to other food such as potatoes, corn, chestnuts.

Sauté
To brown or cook in a small amount of fat. See Fry.

Simmer
To cook in a liquid just below the boiling point, at temperatures of 185°–210°. Bubbles form slowly and collapse below the surface.

Skim
To take away a layer of fat from soup, sauces, etc.

Stock
The liquid in which meat or fish has been boiled together with herbs and vegetables.

Whip
To beat rapidly to produce expansion due to incorporation of air, as applied to cream, eggs, and gelatin dishes.

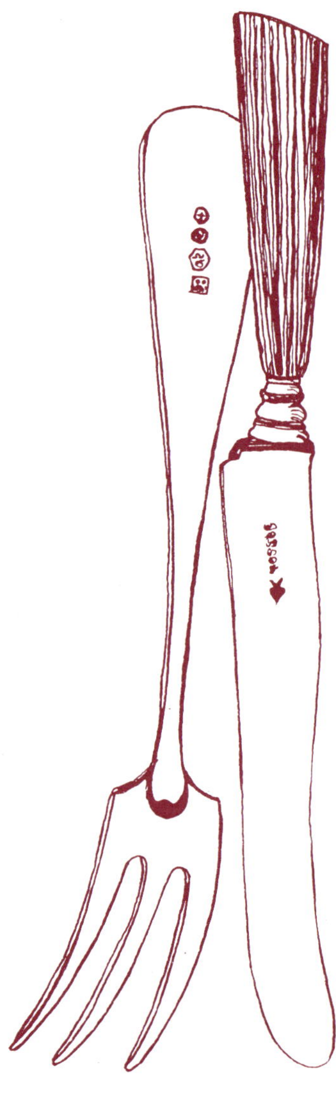

Alphabetical index

English

German

Index by type of dish

English

Salads

Sauces

Soups

Fish dishes

Meat dishes

Poultry and game dishes

Casseroles

Vegetable dishes and dumplings

Pastry

Vegetables dishes and dumplings

Pastry

Desserts

Beverages

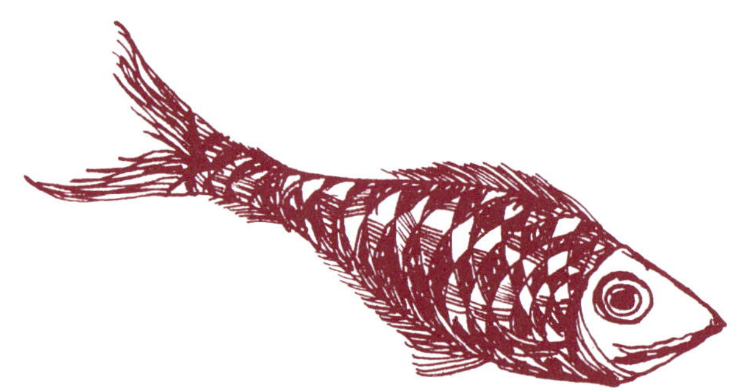